# Socializing on the Spectrum

A resource designed to assist and guide anyone teaching social skills to students with autism.

S. D. Mataia M.ED/SPE

Copyright © 2014 S. D. Mataia M.ED/SPE
All rights reserved.

ISBN: 1494823039
ISBN 13: 9781494823030
Create Space Independent Publishing Platform
North Charleston, South Carolina

# Table of Contents

|  |  |
|---|---|
| 3 | How to use this program |
| 4 | Individualized Plan |
| 5 | 36 Week Unit Plan |
| 7 | Additional Resources |
| 8 | Targeted Skills and Supporting Activities |
| 10 | A Tall Order |
| 11 | A Tall Order (student worksheet) |
| 12 | Accountability Form |
| 13 | Accountability Form (student worksheet) |
| 14 | Being Accountable |
| 15 | Principal Helen Presents: Accountable Ann (student worksheet) |
| 17 | Attentive Body Language |
| 18 | What Attentive Body Language Looks Like (student worksheet) |
| 19 | Being a Good Sport |
| 21 | Being a Good Sport (student worksheet) |
| 22 | Being Attentive |
| 24 | Benefits of Being Accountable |
| 25 | ACCOUNTABLE (student worksheet) |
| 26 | Benefits of Having Good Hygiene |
| 27 | Benefits of Having Good Hygiene (student worksheet) |
| 28 | Bully Bob |
| 29 | Principal Helen Presents: Bully Bob (student worksheet) |
| 32 | Bully Results |
| 33 | Bully Results (student worksheet) |
| 34 | Communicating with Nonverbal Social Cues |
| 35 | Communicating with Nonverbal Social Cues (student worksheet) |
| 36 | Compromise Scenarios |
| 38 | Cooperation Chain |
| 39 | Cooperation Chain (student worksheet) |
| 40 | Coping when Bored |
| 41 | Coping when Bored (student worksheet) |
| 43 | Dealing with a Bully |
| 44 | Dealing with a Bully (student worksheet) |
| 45 | Different Dale |
| 46 | Principal Helen Presents: Different Dale (student worksheet) |
| 48 | Emotional Charades |
| 49 | Empathy |
| 50 | Empathy Worksheet (student worksheet) |
| 51 | Ending War |
| 52 | Ending War (student worksheet) |
| 53 | Expected Stress vs Unexpected Stress |
| 54 | Expected Stress vs Unexpected Stress (student worksheet) |
| 55 | Eye Contact Game |
| 57 | Eye Contact Game (student worksheet) |
| 58 | First Time Asked |
| 59 | First Time Asked (student worksheet) |
| 60 | Get to Know you Interviews |
| 61 | Get to Know you Interviews (student worksheet) |
| 62 | Going with the Flow |
| 63 | Go with the Flow (student worksheet) |
| 65 | Greeting War |
| 66 | Greeting War (student worksheet) |
| 67 | Group Ball Challenge |
| 69 | How do you think they feel? |
| 70 | How do you think they feel? (student worksheet) |
| 71 | How would you feel if? |
| 72 | How would you feel if? (student worksheet) |
| 73 | Hygiene Experiment |
| 74 | I need … |
| 75 | I need … (student worksheet) |
| 76 | Ignoring Negativity |

| | | | |
|---|---|---|---|
| 77 | Interrupt or Wait | 113 | Self-Awareness and Self-Control Questionnaire (student worksheet) |
| 78 | Interrupt or Wait (student worksheet) | | |
| 79 | Jokes: Offensive vs. Not Offensive | 114 | Self-Awareness and Self-Control (student worksheet) |
| 80 | Offensive vs. Not Offensive Jokes (student worksheet) | | |
| | | 115 | Showing Respect |
| 81 | Literal vs. Figurative | 117 | Social Circles |
| 82 | Idioms | 118 | Social Circles (student worksheet) |
| 83 | Lying vs. Being Polite | 119 | Social Games |
| 84 | Lying vs. Being Polite (student worksheet) | 121 | Speed Socializing |
| 85 | Memory Scene | 124 | Spoons |
| 86 | Mock Dinner Party | 125 | Spoons Rules (student worksheet) |
| 89 | Patient Patty | 126 | Spotting Danger |
| 90 | Principal Helen Presents: Patient Patty (student worksheet) | 127 | Spotting Danger (student worksheet) |
| | | 129 | Taking Turns in a Conversation |
| 93 | Positive and Negative Consequences | 131 | Things in Common Circle |
| 94 | Behavior Cycle | 133 | Things in Common Circle (student worksheet) |
| 95 | Positive vs. Negative Consequences | | |
| 96 | Positive vs. Negative Consequences Chart (student worksheet) | 134 | Tone of Voice Game |
| | | 136 | What Could Happen If… |
| 97 | Punctuality | 137 | What Could Happen If… (student worksheet) |
| 99 | Punctuality (student worksheet) | | |
| 100 | Reading Nonverbal Social Cues | 139 | What I like about you |
| 102 | Reading Nonverbal Social Cues (student worksheet) | 141 | What I like about you (student worksheet) |
| | | 142 | What Information is Safe to Share? |
| 103 | Recognizing Emotions | 143 | What Information is Safe to Share? (student worksheet) |
| 104 | Recognizing Emotions (student worksheet) | | |
| | | 144 | Who to approach when you need help |
| 105 | Respect Form | 145 | Who to approach when you need help (student worksheet) |
| 106 | Respect Form (student worksheet) | | |
| 107 | Respectful Ryan | 146 | Whose job is it? |
| 108 | Principal Helen Presents: Respectful Ryan (student worksheet) | 147 | Accountability Roles (student worksheet) |
| | | 148 | Generalization / Practice Ideas for Teachers |
| 110 | Responsibility | | |
| 111 | Responsibility (student worksheet) | 150 | Glossary |
| 112 | Self-Awareness and Self-Control | 154 | Behavior Processing Forms |
| | | 1 62 | Student Social Skills Assessment |

# How to use this program

There are two ways to utilize the lessons in Socializing on the Spectrum. You can target specific social areas by creating an Individualized Plan or follow a 36 Week Unit Plan.

## Individualized Plan

The Individualized Plan is ideal if you have specific social skills you want to target for a specific student or group of students. This plan will allow the instructor to determine the social skills which are most in need of development through the use of the Student Social Skills Assessment. Once the skills are identified, the instructor can then adapt the program in the way that best supports his or her students.

## 36 Week Unit Plan

The 36 Week Unit Plan is ideal for an instructor who would like to teach a variety of social skills throughout a school year. This plan is ideal for a larger group of students who may have varying levels of social skills because it covers 15 different areas of social skills. This plan includes using the Student Social Skills Assessment and allows for instructors to easily set goals and monitor progress in social development areas.

# Individualized Plan

Follow the steps below when using the Individualized Plan.

1. **Complete the Student Social Skills Assessment** (pg. 162) for each student. Be sure to follow the directions and use a specific color to correspond with the date you are completing the assessment.

2. **Review the Student Social Skills Assessments** and determine the areas you want to focus your lessons around. It should be noted that all lessons are still beneficial for kids who have mastered skills. Each lesson is complete with a discussion, so the more the student has mastered the skill, the deeper they will be able to go with the discussion piece.

3. **Use the Targeted Skills and Supporting Activities Chart** (pg. 8) to find the activities that support the areas you want to focus your time on.

4. **Use the Table of Contents** (pg. 1) to locate the activities listed on the Targeted Skills and Supporting Activities Chart

5. **Read the activity directions and implement the activity**. Each Activity Lesson is formatted in the following way:

---

### Title of Activity

Objective and description of activity.

Materials needed (if applicable)

Directions for Activity

---

# 36 Week Unit Plan

| | Accountability | |
|---|---|---|
| Week 1 | **Pre-Assessment (Student Social Skill Assessment)** | Social Games - General Rules pg. 119 |
| Week 2 | Accountable Ann pg. 15 | Benefits of Being Accountable pg. 24 |
| Week 3 | Positive and Negative Consequences pg. 93 | Positive vs. Negative Consequences pg. 95 |
| Week 4 | Responsibility pg. 110 | Whose job is it? pg. 146 |
| | Attention | |
| Week 5 | Attentive Body Language pg. 17 | Eye Contact Game pg. 55 |
| Week 6 | Group Ball Challenge pg. 67 | Social Games - Attention pg. 119 |
| Week 7 | Spoons pg. 124 | Being Attentive pg. 22 |
| Week 8 | First Time Asked pg. 58 | Memory Scene pg. 85 |
| Week 9 | Patient Patty pg. 89 | Taking Turns in a Conversation pg. 129 |
| Week 10 | **Progress Monitoring (Student Social Skill Assessment)** | Social Games - Accountability and Attention pg. 119 |
| | Bullying | |
| Week 11 | Bully Bob pg. 28 | Dealing with a Bully pg. 43 |
| Week 12 | Jokes: Offensive vs. Not Offensive pg. 79 | Social Circles pg. 117 |
| Week 13 | Bully Results pg. 32 | Ignoring Negativity pg. 76 |
| Week 14 | What information is safe to share? pg. 142 | Who to approach when you need help. pg. 144 |
| | Nonverbal Communication | |
| Week 15 | Communicating with Nonverbal Social Cues pg. 38 | Eye Contact Game pg. 55 |
| Week 16 | Reading Nonverbal Social Cues pg. 100 | Emotional Charades pg. 48 |
| | Verbal Communication and Conversations | |
| Week 17 | **Progress Monitoring (Student Social Skill Assessment)** | Get to know you Interviews pg. 60 |

| Week 18 | Taking Turns in a Conversation pg. 129 | Speed Socializing - Greetings and Endings pg. 121 |
| --- | --- | --- |
| Week 19 | I need ….. pg. 74 | Literal vs. Figurative pg. 81 |
| Week 20 | Tone of Voice Game pg. 134 | Speed Socializing - Body Language and taking turns pg. 121 |
| Week 21 | Greeting War pg. 65 and Ending War pg. 51 | Social Games - Verbal and Nonverbal Communication pg. 119 |
| **Understanding Others and Understanding Emotions** | | |
| Week 22 | Different Dale pg. 45 | Empathy pg. 49 |
| Week 23 | How do you think they feel? pg. 69 | Recognizing Emotions pg. 103 |
| **Compromising, Cooperation and Teamwork** | | |
| Week 24 | A Tall Order pg. 10 | Cooperation Chain pg. 38 |
| Week 25 | Social Games - compromising pg. 119 | Compromise Scenarios pg. 36 |
| Week 26 | Group Ball Challenge pg. 67 | **Progress Monitoring (Student Social Skill Assessment)** |
| **Taking Care of Yourself** | | |
| Week 27 | Hygiene Experiment pg.73 | Spotting Danger pg. 126 |
| Week 28 | What Could Happen If… pg. 136 | Benefits of Good Hygiene pg. 26 |
| **Self-Awareness and Self-Control** | | |
| Week 29 | Self-Awareness and Self-Control Questionnaire pg. 113 | Self-Awareness and Self-Control pg. 114 |
| Week 30 | Coping when Bored pg. 40 | Expected vs. Unexpected Stress pg. 53 |
| Week 31 | Going with the flow pg. 62 | Positive and Negative Consequences pg. 93 |
| **Being Polite and Being Respectful** | | |
| Week 32 | Being a Good Sport pg. 23 | Respectful Ryan pg. 107 |
| Week 33 | Interrupt vs. Wait pg. 77 | Mock Dinner Party pg. 86 |
| Week 34 | Punctuality pg. 97 | Lying vs. Being Polite pg. 83 |
| Week 35 | Showing Respect pg. 115 | What I like about you pg. 139 |
| Week 36 | Social Games - Practice all skills learned throughout the year. pg. 119 | **Progress Monitoring (Student Social Skill Assessment)** |

# Additional Resources

## Behavior Processing Forms:

Behavior Processing Forms are located in the back of the book (pg. 147). They are designed to help students process tough situations as well as increase their understanding of the situation, not just show compliance. They can also be used by the instructor as a guide when making social stories for students who may struggle with filling these forms out on their own. Social Stories are a visual way of describing a social lesson through the use of drawings. The purpose of each form is to increase the understanding of social concepts for students.

## Generalization / Practice Ideas:

Generalization and Practice Ideas are located near the back of the book (pg. 141). They are ideas that can be implemented to help reinforce the skills being taught in this program. They provide students with the opportunity to practice the skills they are learning about. Some of the ideas are small things that can be added to a daily routine (ex: requiring your students to hold the door for the person behind them when going out to recess) and other ideas are activities included in the program that work on several skills at once. Some of the activities can be done on a regular basis to promote even more understanding and generalization of social skills (ex: playing social games weekly).

# Targeted Skills and Supporting Activities Chart

After you have used the Social Skills Assessment and have identified the skill areas your students are in need of, use this chart to find activities supporting those skill areas. An activity may be listed in more than one category if it supports more than one skill area. Many activities can be done multiple times.

| Target Skill Area | Supporting Activities |
|---|---|
| **Accountability** | Accountability Form, Accountable Ann, Benefits of Being Accountable, Positive and Negative Consequences, Positive vs. Negative Consequences, Responsibility, Whose job is it? |
| **Attention** | Attentive Body Language, Eye Contact Game, Group Ball Challenge, Spoons, Being Attentive, First Time Asked, Memory Scene, Patient Patty, Taking Turns in a Conversation |
| **Bullying** | Bully Bob, Dealing with a Bully, Jokes, Social Circles, Bully Results, Ignoring Negativity, Safety Form, What Information is safe to share?, Who to approach when you need help |
| **Nonverbal Communication** | Attentive Body Language, Communicating with Nonverbal Social Cues, Eye Contact Game, Reading Nonverbal Social Cues, Emotional Charades |
| **Verbal Communication** | Greeting War, Ending War, Get to know you Interviews, I need…, Literal vs. Figurative, Speed Socializing, Tone of Voice Game |
| **Understanding Others** | Apology Form, Attentive Body Language, Tone of Voice Game, Communicating with Nonverbal Social Cues, Principal Helen Presents Different Dale, Emotional Charades, Empathy, How do you think they feel?, Literal vs. Figurative, Eye Contact Game, Reading Nonverbal Social Cues, Recognizing Emotions |
| **Compromising** | A Tall Order, Cooperation Chain, Social Games, Compromise Scenarios, Group Ball Challenge |

| | |
|---|---|
| **Understanding Emotions** | Communicating with Nonverbal Social Cues, Emotional Charades, Empathy, How would you feel if…, Reading Nonverbal Social Cues, Recognizing Emotions, Tone of Voice Game |
| **Conversations** | Greeting War, Ending War, Literal vs. Figurative, Speed Socializing, Taking Turns in a Conversation |
| **Taking Care of Yourself** | Benefits of Good Hygiene, Coping when Bored, Hygiene Experiment, I need…, Ignoring Negativity, Interrupt or Wait, Whose Job is it?, Responsibility, Self-Awareness and Self-Control Questionnaire, Self-Awareness and Self-Control, Spotting Danger, What Information is safe to share?, Who to approach when you need help, What could happen if… |
| **Self-Awareness and Control** | Self-Awareness and Self-Control Questionnaire, Self-Awareness and Self-Control, Benefits of Being Accountable, Coping when Bored, Expected vs. Unexpected Stress, Going with the flow, how would you feel if…, Patient Patty, Positive vs. Negative Consequences, Positive and Negative Consequences |
| **Being Polite** | Being a Good Sport, Interrupt or Wait, Mock Dinner Party, Punctuality, Social Games, Lying vs. Being Polite |
| **Being Respectful** | Being a Good Sport, Respectful Ryan, Jokes, Punctuality, Respect Form, Showing Respect |
| **Cooperation / Teamwork** | A Tall Order, Being a Good Sport, Cooperation Chain, Social Games, Group Ball Game |
| **Expressing needs** | Cooperation Chain, I need…, Mock Dinner Party, Tone of Voice Game, Who to approach when you need help |
| **Connecting with Others** | Different Dale, Empathy, Eye Contact Game, Get to know you Interviews, What I like about you, Social Circles, Things in Common Circle |
| **Generalization** | A Tall Order, Cooperation Chain, Get to know you Interviews, Group Ball Challenge, Mock Dinner Party, Social Games, Speed Socializing, Generalization / Practice Ideas |

# A Tall Order

<u>Students will practice working together to achieve a common goal.</u>

Materials needed:

- Paper
- Scissors
- Tape or glue
- Paper plates (optional)
- Plastic spoons (optional)

Begin by breaking the class into groups of 3-4 students. Explain to the class ***"the object of this activity is practice the social skills we have been learning, while trying to achieve a common goal with our group."***

The group challenge is to build the tallest free standing tower with the supplies given by the instructor.

Rules:

- The tower must be free standing, meaning no one can support it with anything else, it must stand on its own.
- All groups may only use the supplies given to them by the teacher.
- All groups will receive the same supplies.
- Everyone in your group must help with the process.
- All participants must practice using their social skills (compromise, being polite, sharing, listening, being a good sport, going with the flow, etc…).

When the time limit is up, the instructor will ask all group members to step away from their towers. The instructor will measure each tower and declare a winner. Everyone will practice using a good sport phrase (winners and losers).

Have your students sit in a circle and debrief by asking these questions. Depending on their level of ability, they may use the worksheet to do individually before discussing as a group.

1. Who remembers what the object of the activity was? (**The object of this activity is practice the social skills we have been learning, while trying to achieve a common goal with our group.**)
2. Who thinks they successfully worked on the object of the activity?
3. What things did your group do well together?
4. What things did your group struggle with?
5. What are some changes you could make to improve your success next time?

# A Tall Order

What was the object of this activity?

_____

_____

Was your group successful?

_____

What things did your group do well together?

_____

_____

_____

_____

What things did your group struggle with?

_____

_____

_____

_____

What are some changes you could make to improve your success next time?

_____

_____

_____

_____

# Accountability Form

<u>Students will use this form to help them show and understand accountability for their actions.</u>

The Accountability form can be used when you have a student who is struggling with their role in a situation. The questions are structured to guide them through the situation and help them understand what role they played. This is frequently used after an incident but it could also be used for things such as a student who hasn't handed in homework but doesn't understand why their grade is low or a student who talked through lunch instead of eating and ended up complaining about being hungry in the afternoon. It is meant to be used as a teaching tool and not a punishment.

# Accountability Form

What happened?

___

___

___

___

What role did you play in what happened?

___

___

___

___

Who was affected?

___

___

How do you think it made them feel?

___

___

How do you feel about what happened?

___

___

What should you do differently next time?

___

___

___

# Being Accountable

<u>Students will discuss the meaning and benefits of being accountable.</u>

Start out by discussing the meaning of being accountable. Then read the story, <u>Principal Helen Presents, Accountable Ann</u>. Read through the discussion questions provided to investigate what being accountable means and why it is important to be accountable.

**Accountability:** showing responsibility and ownership for your choices

Some sample reasons why it is important to be accountable:
- Helps others trust you
- Shows you are responsible
- Makes you feel better
- Helps you learn from your mistakes

# Principal Helen Presents: **Accountable Ann**

It was a sunny day at So. Shell Elementary. Mrs. Perry's class had just come inside from recess. Ann always got so thirsty at recess, so she asked if she could fill up her water bottle. Mrs. Perry said, "Yes, but hurry back so you don't miss what we are doing next!"

Ann did just that and hurried back to her seat, after filling up her water bottle. She knew she was supposed to keep her water bottle on the table by the door and not at her seat, but since she was so thirsty and hurried, she didn't get a chance to drink. She decided to sneak her bottle to her seat and placed it under her desk.

Mrs. Perry began to talk to the class about multiplication. Everyone was reciting the times table with Mrs. Perry "2, 4, 6, 8...." Mrs. Perry told us it's easier to remember things when you say them to a beat. She had everyone stand up and push in their chairs. She wanted the class to march in place while saying their times table. Ann didn't realize it at the time, but when she pushed her chair in, it knocked over her water bottle, which then spilled all over the floor where Katie was standing. When Katie began to march in place she slipped and fell. She cried out, "My wrist! My wrist!" When Katie fell she tried to catch herself with her arm and her wrist made a snapping sound as she hit the ground. Ann ran over to help her and noticed the puddle of water and her bottle. She knew what had happened to cause Katie to fall.

She was afraid of disappointing her teacher by not following the rules so she quickly hid the bottle under her sweatshirt. Mrs. Perry ran over to help Katie and had everyone else move away to give her some space. She had a student go ask for help and soon another teacher came to help Katie go see the school nurse.

Later on that day the class found out Katie had broken her wrist. Ann felt terrible! She knew she had caused the accident but was still afraid of disappointing her teacher.

Principal Helen came into the room to talk to the students about accidents. She told the class that accidents aren't always avoidable, but we can do our best to be safe in all situations by being aware of our surroundings and making good choices. Ann couldn't stand the guilt any longer. She raised her hand. "Yes Ann?" said Principal Helen. "Ann's accident was my fault! I should have said something earlier but I was scared" said Ann. "What do you mean it was your fault, Ann?" asked Principal Helen. "I brought my water bottle to my seat when I shouldn't have and it spilled. I was afraid of disappointing Mrs. Perry so I hid the bottle and didn't say anything."

Principal Helen thanked Ann for letting her know. She then turned to the class and said, "Ann just demonstrated a very important skill. Ann was accountable for what she did, even though she was afraid of what would happen."

Ann asked, "What does accountable mean?" Principal Helen went on to say, "Being accountable means you take responsibility for your choices. It means you don't let someone else take the blame for something you did and most of all it means being responsible for yourself." "Oh, I see" said Ann. Why would someone choose to not be accountable if it is all of those good things?" Principal Helen replied, "Well, just like you were afraid, others are often afraid as well. They don't want to get in trouble, they don't want anyone to be mad at them, and they don't want to disappoint others. When you are accountable for your choices people start to trust you more, and generally people will admire you, even if your choice wasn't the best one you could have made." "Yeah, that's true. I was afraid at first but I realized it was the right thing to do and it did make me feel better to just be honest about it" Ann said. "Doing the right thing almost always makes you feel better in the long run. Even when it's difficult to do." said Principal Helen.

Discussion Questions:

1. What does being accountable mean?
2. Why wasn't Ann accountable at first?
3. What made Ann choose to be accountable?
4. What was the outcome of choosing to be accountable in this situation?
5. Do you have any examples of a time when you were scared but choose to be accountable for what you did?
6. How do you feel after being accountable?

# Attentive Body Language

<u>Students will identify how different parts of the body should look when paying attention.</u>

**Attention:** where a person's focus and interest is directed

Begin by discussing the meaning of attention and then describing some situations where you would need to have an attentive body language. Ask your students if they can think of any situations.

Some possible answers are:

- When listening to your teacher give directions
- When someone is talking to you
- When you meet someone new and do introductions
- When you are leaving and saying bye to someone

Next, talk about why it is important to use attentive body language. Ask your students to brainstorm some reasons.

Some possible answers are:

- To understand what others are saying to you better
- To be respectful
- To show you are listening
- To see the messages the person talking is giving with their body language

Have the students fill out the "What attentive body language looks like" worksheet and then discuss as a class.

# What Attentive Body Language Looks Like

Describe what attentive eyes look like.
_____
_____

Describe what an attentive mouth should look like.
_____
_____

Describe what attentive hands should look like.
_____
_____

Describe what attentive legs should look like.
_____
_____

Describe what attentive feet should look like.
_____
_____

What are some things you could do with your body that would make you look like you ARE NOT paying attention?
_____
_____
_____
_____

# Being a Good Sport

Students will discuss and brainstorm how to be a good sport in different situations.

Materials needed:
- Board games

**Good Sport:** a person who is able to win or lose without putting others down

Discuss the meaning of the phrase *good sport* with your class. Read the following to your class after introducing the topic.

*"Most people enjoy playing games and having fun. Most games involve a winner and a loser. In order to keep a game enjoyable, the participants need to be good sports. Whether someone wins or loses the game, they have responsibility in keeping the game fun by being considerate of how the other person is feeling while playing. It's easy for some people to become competitive while playing. Being competitive is fine as long as you aren't losing the purpose of the game, which is often to do your best and enjoy what you are doing. Whether you win or lose you can and should be enjoying the game."*

As a class, list some scenarios where it would be important to be a good sport.

Some possible answers are:

- Board games
- Video games
- Sports

- Challenges
- Science Fair

As a class, list some good sport comments someone could make if they win a game or competition. Also make a list of good sport comments someone could make if they lose a game or competition.

Some possible answers are:

| Good Sport Comments from the Winner | Good Sport Comment from the Loser |
|---|---|
| • Everyone played really hard | • Good game |
| • Nice game | • Congratulations |
| • You were a tough competitor | • You played really well |
| • Our whole team played really hard | • Let's play again sometime |
| • Let's play again | • Great Job |

Now comes the fun part! Allow your students to spend the remaining time playing games together and practicing their good sport skills. Remind them the point of the activity is to practice being a good sport.

# Being a Good Sport

**Write down some phrase a good sport could use if they were winning and phrases they could use if they were losing.**

| Good Sport Comments from the **Winner** | Good Sport Comment from the **Loser** |
|---|---|
|  |  |
|  |  |
|  |  |
|  |  |
|  |  |
|  |  |
|  |  |
|  |  |

# Being Attentive

<u>Students will practice paying attention to verbal and nonverbal actions.</u>

This activity takes a little work on the instructor's part. The instructor will tell the students they are going to read a story as a class and then quizzed after. They will tell the students the goal is for the students to pay close attention so they can get as many questions right as possible. As the instructor reads the story they will also complete the actions in parentheses. The students are NOT told the quiz will be on comprehension as well as visual observations.

Read the following story:

*One day a lady was walking down the street to go to the store. As she walked, she noticed another person out walking her dog. It was a beautiful dog with golden brown hair.*

*The dog reminded the lady of when she was young and had a dog of her own. (touch your nose) She thought back to how she used to take her dog for walks and play Frisbee with him at the park. (touch your earlobe) Her dog was named Charlie. Charlie was her best friend as a child. She thought about a time when Charlie and she went on a hike. (put your hand on the top of your head) Charlie was a very good listener and would always stay right by the lady's side.*

*On this particular day Charlie took off running, which was very unlike him. The lady had thought about how bizarre it was for Charlie to do this. (tough your nose again) She called his name but he didn't come. As she kept walking she noticed him stopped up ahead and looking at something. The lady ran to Charlie and saw he was standing over a young boy who had fallen and hurt himself. The lady felt relieved to find Charlie but also upset that the boy was hurt. She went to call for help and the boy was saved.*

Questions:

- What color was the dog in the story?
- What was the name of the dog in the story?
- What made the lady think of the dog?
- How many times did the instructor touch their nose?

Read the story again and ask these questions the second time:

- How many characters are in the story?
- How many times did the instructor touch their ear lobe?
- How many times did the instructor touch their head?
- Bonus Question: How many times was the name Charlie used in the story? (8)

Discuss the purpose of the activity with your students. The purpose of this activity was to point out that there are many more details going on than we realize. When you don't give your full attention, you are likely to be missing things.

# Benefits of Being Accountable

Students will investigate and list the benefits of being accountable.

This activity should be done after the other accountability activities so the students have more prior knowledge to draw from.

Begin by reviewing the meaning of being accountable.

**Accountability**: showing responsibility for your choices

Ask your students to give examples of a time they showed accountability. Ask them to describe how they felt after being accountable.

After discussing this topic as a class, make a list together of the benefits to being accountable.

Possible answers could be:

- Feel less guilt
- Show people you are trustworthy
- Learn from your mistakes
- Not getting others in trouble for something you did
- Showing you are responsible
- Not relying on others as much

Once you have discussed accountability and its benefits, have your students fill out the ACCOUNTABILITY poem by trying to think of a benefit of being accountable for each letter in the word or something they are accountable for doing. (ex: acting appropriate, carrying their bag, etc...)

A _____

C _____

C _____

O _____

U _____

N _____

T _____

A _____

B _____

L _____

E _____

# Benefits of Having Good Hygiene

Students will explore the benefits of taking care of their bodies and health.

Review the meaning of hygiene.

**Hygiene:** keeping a clean, healthy body with a clean personal appearance

Once your students have a basic understanding of what hygiene means, use the "Benefits of Having Good Hygiene?" worksheet. Use this worksheet to either discuss topics as a group or have students individually fill out and then talk about together.

Some possible answers are:

- Fresh breath
- Whiter teeth
- Smell better
- Look nice
- Clothes last longer
- People are more likely to want to be around you
- Clean and shiny hair
- Stay healthier
- Feel better about yourself

# Benefits to Having Good Hygiene

Answer the questions about hygiene by trying to think about what could happen in each scenario.

- What is a benefit of brushing your teeth?

_____
_____

- What is a benefit of wearing clean clothes?

_____
_____

- What is a benefit of washing your hands?

_____
_____

- What is a benefit of washing your hair regularly?

_____
_____

- What is a benefit of showering or bathing regularly?

_____
_____

- What is a benefit of wearing socks with your tennis shoes?

_____
_____

- What is a benefit of wearing deodorant?

_____
_____

- What is a benefit of brushing your hair?

_____
_____

- What are the benefits of having good hygiene?

_____
_____

# Bully Bob

Students will read a story about bullying and discuss issues concerning bullies.

Begin by asking your students if they know what a bully is? Tell them the definition of a bully.

**Bully:** a person who tries to intimidate or mistreat someone they interpret to be weaker than them

Read the Story, Principal Helen Presents, Bully Bob to the class and talk about the discussion questions at the end.

# Principal Helen Presents: **Bully Bob**

*Bob looked like any other kid in the third grade. He often wore his favorite t-shirt with his favorite pair of jeans. He loved eating dessert first and playing in the dirt. Yes, Bob looked like any other kid, but Bob had a secret. A secret that affected him greatly but one he didn't want anyone to find out about.*

*Bob lived with his Mom, Dad, and big brother, Frank. His Uncle Dan also lived with him. Bob's Uncle Dan was down on his luck. He lost his job and had no money to live on his own. Bob noticed his Uncle was often mad. His uncle would frequently take out his anger on Bob by calling him terrible names. Bob was afraid to tell anyone but began to feel bad about himself. He began to think the things his uncle would tell him were true.*

*One day when Bob was at school, he noticed there was a kid in his class who always got A's. His name was Levi. When Bob would look at his own grades and see he wasn't doing well, it would make him feel even worse to see Levi getting such good grades. One day he was feeling so badly about himself that he started to make fun of Levi and call him names. Levi didn't know what to do. He ran to the bathroom and started to cry.*

*Later on Bob saw another kid Troy, who always read faster than Bob did in class. Bob made faces whenever he would read and started calling him names too. Troy noticed him doing this but decided to ignore him. Bob noticed many of his classmates had started to avoid him. This made Bob feel even worse, which he then took out on others.*

*Bob noticed he didn't have any friends anymore. He overheard kids calling him Bob the Bully one day. This made him feel sad which he again, took out on those around him. He tripped the girl walking by him in the hall and yelled at her friend. Bob's parents were called and he was sent to talk to the principal.*

*Bob had felt bad about all of the things he had done, but felt worse about himself.*

*He had started to believe the things his uncle had been telling him. He broke down and started crying when his parents came in. Bob's parents had no idea he was feeling this way and that his uncle was saying those things to him.*

*Principal Helen explained to Bob that his behavior was known as bullying and often bullies were people with low self-confidence. They feel so bad and don't know how to deal with it, so they end up taking it out on those around them. When someone becomes a bully it's very hard for them to make any real friends."*

*This was not the person Bob wanted to be. He asked Principal Helen how he could make things better. Principal Helen explained to Bob that he would have to earn the trust of his classmates back by first apologizing and then showing them he was really much nicer than he had been acting.*

*Bob's parents spoke with his uncle about the situation and told him if he too didn't make things better, then he would have to move out. His uncle felt terrible and said he didn't realize how his comments were affecting Bob.*

*Both Bob and his Uncle turned over a new leaf that day and started to treat others how they wanted to be treated. That change alone made both of them start to feel better about themselves.*

## Discussion Questions:

1. What do you think self-confidence is?

2. How do you think Levi handled being bullied?

3. How do you think Troy handled being bullied?

4. Why do you think Bob was acting like a bully?

5. Why do you think Bob's Uncle was acting like a bully?

6. What did Bob and his Uncle do at the end of the story that made them start to feel better about themselves?

7. Have you ever felt like you were being bullied?

8. Have you ever done anything to act like a bully?

9. What are some positive things you can do if you are being bullied?

10. What are some positive things you can do if you think you are acting like a bully?

# Bully Results

<u>Students will discuss what can happen when someone bullies someone else.</u>

Review the necessary vocab word for this activity. This activity should be done after Dealing with a Bully and Bully Bob so the students have more prior knowledge to draw from.

**Bully:** a person who tries to intimidate or mistreat someone they interpret to be weaker than them

Talk about some of the causes for bullying and brainstorm how bullies may feel as well as how the person being bullied may feel.

Read the following:

*"Sometimes people who bully others do so because they don't feel very good about themselves. Having low self-esteem can be caused by several things, but it also can cause the person who is feeling badly to take it out on others around them. It is important to remember that if someone is bullying you, it doesn't reflect what kind of person you are, it's more likely to reflect how that person is feeling about themself. If you ever feel like someone is bullying you or you feel unsafe, it is important to tell an adult you trust."*

Have your students fill out the "Bully Results" worksheet and then discuss together as a class.

# Bully Results

How do you think a bully feels when they bully someone?

_____     _____
_____     _____
_____     _____

How do you think a person being bullied feels?

_____     _____
_____     _____
_____     _____

Fill in the circle for all of the positive choices you could make if you were being bullied.

- ○ Tell an adult you trust
- ○ Ignore the person who is bullying you
- ○ Tell the person to stop treating you that way
- ○ Tell the person how they are making you feel

Draw a picture of someone being bullied who is using a positive bully strategy

```
┌─────────────────────────────────────────────────────────┐
│                                                         │
│                                                         │
│                                                         │
│                                                         │
└─────────────────────────────────────────────────────────┘
```

# Communicating with Nonverbal Social Cues

<u>Students will practice communicating using only nonverbal social cues.</u>

Begin by explaining what nonverbal social cues are.

**Nonverbal Social Cues:** information given by a person through their body language and facial expressions, rather than the words being spoken

The instructor will challenge the group to accomplish certain task by only using nonverbal social cues. They are not allowed to speak verbally at all.

Challenges:
- Line up in alphabetical order by your first name.
- Line up in alphabetical order by your middle name.
- Line up in order of your age.
- Line up in order of your birth<u>day</u> (not year).
- Line up in alphabetical order of the town you were born in.
- Line up in order of how many pets you have.
- Line up in order of height.

After the activities are completed ask these questions to your class:
1. Were you able to accomplish the tasks without speaking verbally?
2. What challenges did you face together as a team?
3. What things did you do well together as a team?
4. What could you and your team do next time to communicate even better?

# Communicating with Nonverbal Social Cues

Were you able to accomplish the tasks without speaking verbally?

_____

_____

What challenges did you face together as a team?

_____

_____

_____

_____

What things did you do well together as a team?

_____

_____

_____

_____

What could you and your team do next time to communicate even better?

_____

_____

_____

_____

# Compromise Scenarios

<u>Students will practice identifying and problem solving situations that require compromise.</u>

Begin by discussing what it means to compromise.

**Compromise:** when two sides give in a little and meet in the middle

Next discuss the importance of compromise. Read the following:

*"Compromising is important because it helps keep everyone happy and helps everyone be heard. When people compromise, no one feels as though their perspective or thoughts don't matter. By compromising you can also learn new ways to do things and sometimes you may learn better ways to do things."*

Read the following scenarios to your students and discuss possible compromises they could make if they were in these situations.

- You are playing a card game with some of your friends and are used to playing with a different set of rules than they are using. What could you do to compromise?

- You are working on an art project in class and you need a turquoise marker to complete your picture but you see there is only one left and someone else is using it. What could you do to compromise?

- You are working on an art project in class and you notice someone needs a turquoise marker to complete their picture but you are using the only one left. What could you do to compromise?

- There are no assigned seats at lunch but you still have a favorite spot to sit. Just as you go to sit down, someone else is also about to sit there. What could you do to compromise?

After discussing the scenarios and possible compromises, discuss the following questions:

1. Were you able to come up with a compromise for each situation?
2. What was difficult about compromising?
3. What are some positives to compromising?
4. Why do you think it's important to know how to compromise?
5. Are you good at compromising or is it hard for you to do?
6. Do you have any examples to share about a time when you compromised with someone?

# Cooperation Chain

<u>Students will work together to accomplish a goal and practice social skills they've learned.</u>

Materials needed:

- Construction paper
- Scissors
- Glue sticks

Start by splitting the students into groups of 3-4. Read the object of the activity as it is written: ***"The object of the activity is for you to work together appropriately to achieve a common goal."***

The challenge is to work together to create as long of a chain as possible in a given time period (chosen by instructor).

Rules:

- All group members are <u>only allowed to use one hand the entire time</u>.
- Each group will be given an equal amount of supplies.
- The teacher can select whatever amount of time works well for the class.
- The groups are only allowed to use the materials the teacher gave them.
- The longest chain at the end of the time period, wins!

Questions to talk about after completing activity.

1. Who remembers what the object of the activity was? (The object of the activity is for you to work together appropriately to achieve a common goal.)

2. How many people think they achieved the object of the activity?

3. What social skills did your group use to help you be successful?

4. What struggles did your group have?

5. What social skills could you have used to make your group more successful?

6. What are some social lessons you learned from this activity?

# Cooperation Chain

1. What was the object of this activity? How many people think they achieved the object of the activity?

   _____
   _____

2. What social skills did your group use to help you be successful?

   _____
   _____

3. What struggles did your group have?

   _____
   _____

4. What social skills could you have used to make your group more successful?

   _____
   _____

5. What are some social lessons you learned from this activity?

   _____
   _____

# Coping When Bored

<u>Students will talk about what to do and what not to do when bored.</u>

Review the necessary vocab words for this lesson.

**Bored:** not being interested in what is happening around you

**Coping**: appropriately dealing with a difficult feeling

Introduce the lesson by reading the following.

*"Have you ever been bored when someone was talking to you? Of course you have! Everyone gets bored sometimes. You may even be bored as I am saying this. The truth is that boredom happens at times. Believe it or not, I'm sure people even get bored listening to you talk sometimes. It's ok though because it happens to everyone. It's important to respond appropriately when you are bored in order to not hurt other's feelings. We wouldn't want someone to be rude if they were bored by us, so we need to be respectful of their feelings too."*

As a class, brainstorm some things you could do when you are bored. Discuss situations that involve not being rude to someone else just because you are bored.

Have your students look at the "Coping When Bored" worksheet. Depending on their academic level, either look at each scene and talk about them together or have them first fill it out on their own and then talk about it as a class.

# Coping When Bored

Read each scenario and then brainstorm an appropriate way you could cope with being bored in that situation.

Your teacher is helping you with your work, even though you don't want to do it. How could you cope with being bored?

_____
_____
_____

Your older sister wants to tell you about her day. You are not interested. How could you cope with being bored? _____
_____
_____

You really want to go outside and play but there is a lightning storm. How could you cope with being bored? _____
_____
_____
_____

Your dad wants to talk to you about something but you are not interested. How could you cope with being bored? _____
_____
_____
_____

You really want to play with your new video game but you have to finish your chores first. How could you could you cope with being bored?
_____
_____
_____

You are supposed to go meet your friends to play at the park but you have to finish your homework before you can go. How could you cope with being bored?
_____
_____
_____

You are going camping with your family, but the car ride is 2 hours long. How could you cope with being bored? _____
_____
_____

# Dealing with a Bully

<u>Students will learn some strategies to use if they encounter a bully.</u>

Review the necessary vocab word for this activity.

**Bully:** a person who tries to intimidate or mistreat someone they interpret to be weaker than them

Read through the "Dealing with a Bully" worksheet with your students and explain the different possible strategies to use when encountering a bully.
Discuss different social cues to look for when deciding what strategy to use.

Bully Strategies:

**Inquire:** Ask them why they would say or do what they said or did.

**Pretend it doesn't bother you:** Say something like, "Thanks, I try!"

**Be assertive**: Say, "I want you to stop doing or saying that"

**Ignore:** Don't acknowledge what they say and walk away.

**Let them know how you feel:** Tell them they are hurting your feelings or making you feel bad when they say or do those types of things.

**Be sure to emphasize to your students to tell an adult they trust if someone is bullying them and making them feel unsafe.**

# Dealing with a Bully

**Bully Strategies:**

**Inquire:** Ask them why they would say or do what they said or did.

**Pretend it doesn't bother you:** Say something like, "Thanks, I try!"

**Be assertive**: Say, "I want you to stop doing or saying that"

**Ignore:** Don't acknowledge what they say and walk away.

**Let them know how you feel:** Tell them they are hurting your feelings or making you feel bad when they say or do those types of things.

---

**Write a bully strategy (listed above) that could be used to deal with the bully actions described below.**

Someone says: "You need to lose weight."

Someone pulls your chair out from under you as you were about to sit down.

Someone calls you a nose picker and laughs at you.

Someone makes fun of your parents.

Someone is throwing small pieces of paper at you when the teacher isn't looking.

Someone calls you a tattle tale.

Someone copies everything you say and won't stop.

**What should you do if you are ever feeling unsafe because of a bully?**

# Different Dale

Students will practice looking at and being accepting of differences in people.

Start by discussing what it means to be accepting of others.

**Accepting others:** appreciating someone for who they are and not trying to change them or make fun of them for being different from you

Read the story, Principal Helen Presents, Different Dale and talk about the discussion questions at the end.

# Principal Helen Presents: **Different Dale**

*Dale is a fifth grader at So. Shell Elementary. Dale is a good looking kid. He has thick black hair with big dark eyes and athletic build. Dale is always well dressed and clean but something is different about Dale.*

*Dale tends to keep to himself and makes motions with his body that are unlike the other students. He often rocks back and forth and flaps his hands in the air when he gets excited. When things don't go the way Dale expects, he can become very loud. Sometimes he needs to leave the classroom to calm down.*

*I often wonder why Dale acts the way he does. I want to be friends with him but I am afraid I might make him yell. I noticed Dale is very good at building things. I love watching him build things and want to join in, but I'm pretty sure he doesn't want me to. So I just stay back and watch.*

*One day I saw some kids making fun of Dale. I wasn't sure what to do or if Dale even noticed they were making fun of him. I couldn't stop thinking about it, so I decided to talk to Principal Helen. Principal Helen explained to me that, although Dale may do things differently than the other students, he still has feelings and wants friends. She told me Dale has a hard time talking to other kids and didn't know how to ask them to play. Principal Helen said she thinks it's wonderful that I am interested in Dale and that I'm able to look past his different behaviors and see him as someone fun to play with. I thanked Principal Helen and went home.*

*The next day I decided I would try to play with Dale if he began to build things. Sure enough, he started building another amazing structure. I approached Dale and asked if he cared if I watched him build. He said sure and continued to build. I noticed a pattern of blocks Dale would choose, so I started to organize the unused blocks for him to make it easier for him to grab. Principal Helen walked by and gave me a wink and a smile and I knew I had done something great! I was happy to make a new friend who has such an amazing ability to build things.*

Discussion Questions:

1. What are some of the things that are different about Dale?
2. How is Dale similar to the other kids?
3. Why do you think Dale was playing by himself most of the time?
4. Why do you think Dale would become loud at times?
5. Do you know anyone who acts different than you expect or are used to?
6. Is there anything you do that other people might think is different?
7. Do you want to have friends?
8. Do you think Dale wants to have friends?
9. Do you think Dale knew the kids were making fun of him?
10. What did the student do at the end of the story that was so great?
11. Would you or have you ever done anything like that before?

# Emotional Charades

<u>Students will practice recognizing different emotions in themselves and others.</u>

Emotional Charades is similar to regular charades, only students are acting out emotions instead of words or phrases. The instructor will give an emotion to a student and they will act as if they are feeling that emotion. The other students will guess what the emotion is. Whoever guesses correctly gets to go next. Some emotions can look very similar so you can make it a little easier by being a narrator and setting the scene or displaying a list of emotions for the students to choose from when guessing. For beginning levels, the instructor can act out the emotions and the students can do all of the guessing.

Some ideas for emotions to act out are:

| | | |
|---|---|---|
| Sad | Shy | Proud |
| Happy | Confused | Disappointed |
| Exhausted | Overwhelmed | Misunderstood |
| Depressed | Bored | Confused |
| Stressed | Scared | Ecstatic |
| Anxious | Concerned | Content |
| Excited | Worried | Satisfied |
| Nervous | Accomplished | Irritable |

# Empathy

<u>Students will practice recognizing and understanding how others feel.</u>

This activity requires a movie. Pick out any age appropriate movie that has characters with relatable situations to your students (most Disney movies for kids would work). Start by discussing what empathy is.

**Empathy:** the ability to understand and share the feelings of another

Be sure to emphasize that you don't need to have gone through a similar situation to have empathy for someone. Let your students know you will be watching a movie and you want them to focus on a particular character throughout the movie (it works to show a clip as well if you don't have a long time period). Use the empathy worksheet to discuss how the character was feeling during the movie and how you knew they were feeling that way. Depending on your student's level, you can either just discuss the questions or have them fill it out first and then discuss together. Either way the important piece is discussing it together.

VARIATIONS:

The level of this activity can be changed by the choice of video shown and the depth of discussion that is had. For younger children, the discussion can be less in depth by choosing characters with more obvious nonverbal cues, like tears or yelling. For higher level kids, choose characters with more subtle social cues, like folding arms or having slumped over posture.

# Empathy Worksheet

What is the name of your character?
_____

Describe a scene from the movie and then describe how your character felt during that scene.

Scene:
_____
_____
_____
_____

Character's feelings :
_____
_____
_____
_____

What were some verbal clues they gave to help you understand how they were feeling? (Words, Tone of Voice)
_____
_____
_____
_____

What were some visual clues they gave to help you understand how they were feeling? (Body Language)
_____
_____
_____
_____

How would you want someone to respond to you if you were feeling the way your character was feeling?
_____
_____
_____
_____

# Ending War

<u>Students will increase their vocabulary of different types of endings to a conversation.</u>

Ending war is similar to the card game War, in that each player goes back and forth until someone wins. In Ending War, there are two players and each player will say something you would say to end a conversation, without repeating, until someone can't think of one. If you are caught not being able to think of an ending then you lose that round. You can start fresh with the endings each round. Whoever wins the most rounds wins.

The instructor can start the activity by explaining in depth what an ending to a conversation is and what purpose it serves. If you need assistance you can read the sample below.

*"Endings are used to end a conversation. It is considered very rude to just walk away when you are done talking to someone. In order to not offend others and to let the other person you are talking to know you are done talking, it is important to learn about endings. Endings should be done by everyone participating in a conversation in order to politely signal the conversation is over."*

Some examples of endings are:
- "It's been nice talking to you."
- "It was nice to meet you."
- "Bye"
- "See you later"
- "Audios"
- Have a good night!
- Have a good day!

# Ending War

Make a list of as many endings to a conversation as you can think of.

# Expected Stress vs. Unexpected Stress

Students will explore the difference between different types of stress.

Review the necessary vocabulary words for this lesson.

**Stress:** strain that can be felt mentally, emotionally or physically

**Expected:** things you can predict happening

**Unexpected:** things you can't predict happening

Discuss how stress can affect a person by reading the following:

*"Stress is something everyone experiences at some time. It can make you feel yucky and can even make some people sick. It is important to learn how to identify stress and learn how to handle it appropriately."*

Have your students complete the "Expected Stress vs. Unexpected Stress" worksheet. Once they are finished, discuss the worksheet together as a group. Brainstorm some ideas as a class for dealing with stressful situations appropriately.

Some possible answers are:

- Taking deep breaths
- Sing a soothing song in your head
- Take a break
- Get a drink of water
- Listen to some music
- Count to 10
- Go for a short walk (with permission)
- Use a fidget
- Talk to someone about what is bothering you

# Expected Stress vs. Unexpected Stress

Mark an **E** on the line next to the stresses that can be expected and mark a **U** on the line next to the stresses that are unexpected.

_____ Getting stuck in traffic

_____ Having homework

_____ The schedule changing

_____ Having a substitute teacher because your teacher is sick

_____ The lunch room being noisy

_____ Having to stay inside for recess because it started to rain

_____ Having to do work you don't like to do at school

_____ Having a fire drill

_____ Your computer freezing up when you are using it

_____ Your favorite snack missing from the vending machine

_____ Thunder and lightening

_____ Spilling your lunch on the floor by accident

_____ Someone in your class getting hurt and crying loudly

_____ Your favorite toy breaking

_____ Having to give a presentation at school

What are some ways you can appropriately handle an expected stress?

_____

_____

_____

What are some ways you can appropriately handle an unexpected stress?

_____

_____

_____

# Eye Contact Game

## Students will practice using eye contact to communicate.

The instructor will break the group into pairs and then read the directions below to the class:

*"We are going to play, Secret Agent Looks. This is a game where each group has a secret agent in it. The secret agent will be told a secret location he or she need to get his or her partner to in order to be safe, however, if someone sees the secret agent telling anyone where the secret location is, the secret agent will be caught. The secret agent is only allowed to communicate using eye contact and nodding yes or no. If they use any other body language or verbal language then the group will be caught and sent back to the beginning to start over. The group that successfully has their secret agent get them to the safe location first will win! Now let's practice signaling using only our eyes.* (Teacher demonstrates using eyes to direct someone) *then let's use our head to say yes and no* (teacher demonstrates).

The instructor should ask if there are any questions and then gather the secret agents to disclose the secret location. Once everyone is at the starting point, the game can begin. Remember to talk about the discussion questions after the activity.

(Discussion questions on the next page)

At the end of the game discuss the questions below together as a class:

1. Were you able to successfully get your partners to the secret locations?
2. What were some challenges your group faced?
3. What were some things your group did well together?
4. What could you do to be more successful next time?
5. Why is it important to look at someone's eyes when you are communicating with them?

# Eye Contact Game

Were you able to successfully get your partners to the secret locations?

_____

What were some challenges your group faced?

_____

_____

What were some things your group did well together?

_____

_____

What could you do to be more successful next time?

_____

_____

Why is it important to look at someone's eyes when you are communicating with them?

_____

_____

# First Time Asked

<u>Students will look at the importance of following directions the first time they are asked</u>

The First Time Asked form can be used when you have a student who is struggling with following directions the first time they are asked. The questions are structured to guide them through the situation and help them understand why it's important to follow directions the first time they are given.

This form is meant to be used as a teaching tool and not a punishment.

# First Time Asked

What direction did you not follow the first time?

_____
_____

Why didn't you follow the direction the first time it was given?

_____
_____

What did you do instead of following directions?

_____
_____

Who did it affect?

_____
_____

How did it affect them?

_____
_____

What should you have done?

_____
_____

Why is it important to follow directions?

_____
_____

# Get to Know You Interviews

<u>Students will practice strategies used when getting to know someone else.</u>

Begin this activity by reading the following to the class:

*"Getting to know others can be a tough skill for some people. They may not know what to say or may be nervous about what the other person will say. The fear of not knowing what will happen is enough to keep some people from even trying to get to know others. As with many other things, practice helps us improve our skills. So during this activity we are going to practice getting to know each other better."*

As a class, brainstorm some reasons why it is beneficial to get to know other people. Some possible answers are:

- Make more friends
- Find out things you have in common
- Have more people to ask for help if you need
- Learn new things
- Learn new perspectives

Have your students pair up, preferably with someone they don't talk to a lot. Give each student a copy of the "Get to know you Interview" worksheets and have them choose at least 10 questions from the sheet to ask the other person.

After everyone has completed their interviews with their partners, the students will take turns presenting what they learned about their partner to the class. Remind students to practice being a good listener when others are talking. This includes looking at the speaker, being quiet, smiling and head nodding at times.

# Get to Know You Interview

Choose at least 10 questions from the list below to ask your partner. Be sure to write down their answers so you can tell the class what you learned about them.

- Where do you live?
- Where were you born?
- How old are you?
- When is your birthday?
- What is your favorite thing to do?
- What is your favorite book?
- What is your favorite movie?
- What is your favorite thing to eat?
- What is your favorite holiday?
- What is something you are really good at?
- What is something you are not good at?
- What is your favorite color?
- What is your middle name?
- What is your favorite subject in school?
- What do you want to be when you grow up?
- Do you have any pets?
- If you have pets, what kind and how many?
- If you could go anywhere on vacation where would you go?
- If you could have any super power, what super power would you want?
- How many siblings do you have?
- How tall are you?
- What kind of music do you like?
- What is your favorite song?
- What is your favorite number?
- What is your favorite sport?
- What is your favorite instrument?

# Going with the flow

<u>Students will brainstorm what to do when a situation doesn't go as planned.</u>

**Stress:** Strain that can be felt mentally, emotionally or physically

Review the meaning of stress and then read the following to your class:

*"Even if we plan out our days, it is likely things won't always go exactly as planned. This can cause a lot of stress at times because you may not know what to do when things aren't what you expected. When this happens you have two choices. You can fight it and get really upset, which generally doesn't change anything, or you can come up with another plan to get you through the situation. It isn't always easy to change plans quickly, especially if what you were planning on doing was something fun that you were looking forward to. Learning to go with the flow and adapt to changes will help you enjoy your day better even if it isn't what you expected. As with many other things, practice helps improve this skill."*

Give your students a "Go with the flow" worksheet and ask them to brainstorm a new idea to solve the problem faced in the pictures. Once everyone is done, have the class share their ideas aloud.

# Go with the flow

Brainstorm a new plan for the situations in the pictures below.

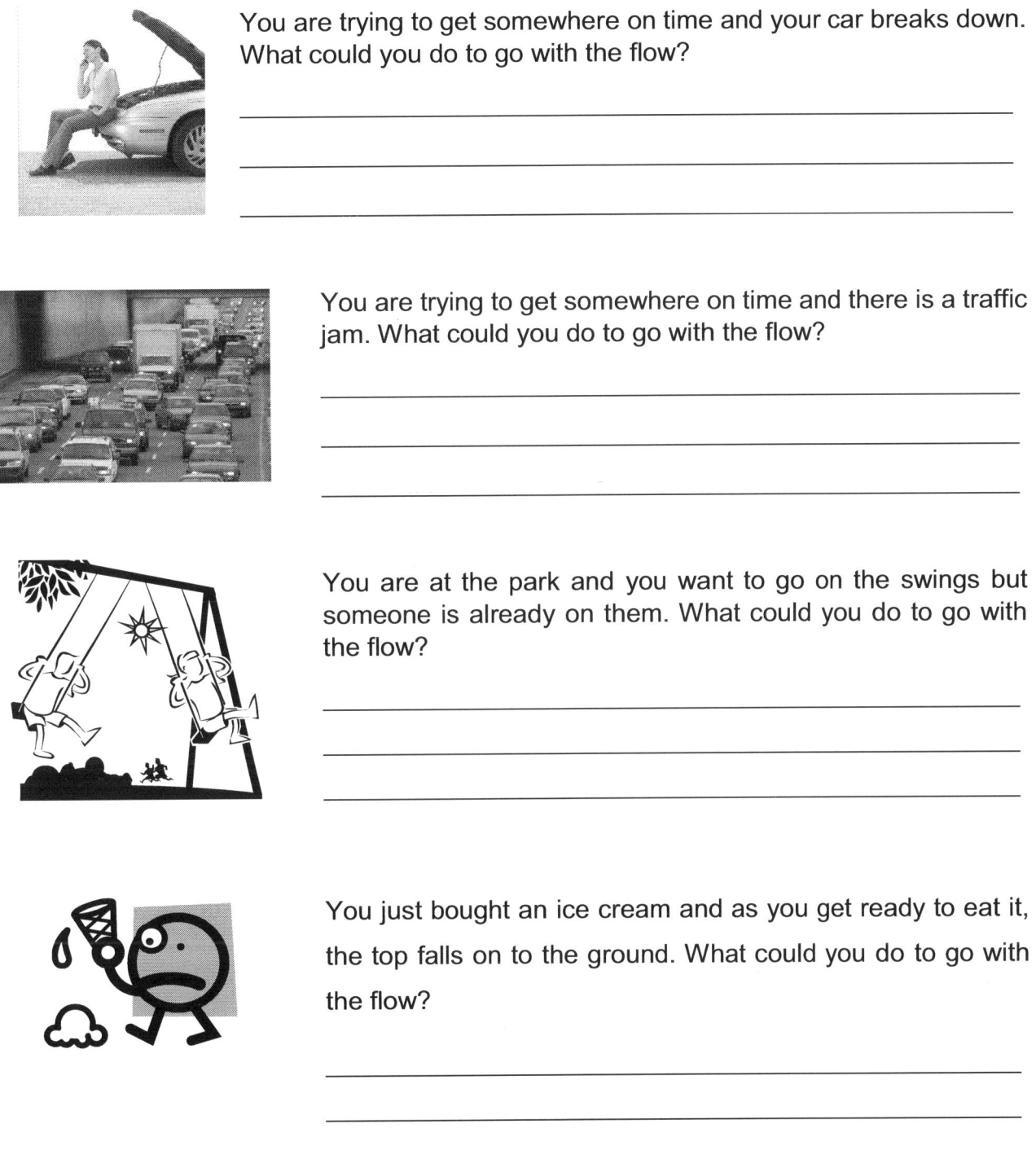

You are trying to get somewhere on time and your car breaks down. What could you do to go with the flow?

_____
_____
_____

You are trying to get somewhere on time and there is a traffic jam. What could you do to go with the flow?

_____
_____
_____

You are at the park and you want to go on the swings but someone is already on them. What could you do to go with the flow?

_____
_____
_____

You just bought an ice cream and as you get ready to eat it, the top falls on to the ground. What could you do to go with the flow?

_____
_____
_____

You are walking outside and it starts to rain. What could you do to go with the flow?

_____
_____
_____

You want to go see a movie but when you go to buy tickets you see there is a really long line. What could you do to go with the flow?

_____
_____
_____

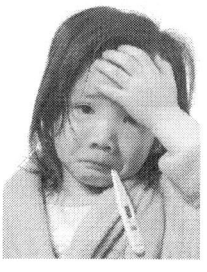

You are supposed to go to the fair and go on rides but you woke up feeling yucky. What could you do to go with the flow?

_____
_____
_____

Describe a time when things didn't go the way you wanted them to. What was your response? What could you do in the future to go with the flow during that type of situation?

_____
_____
_____
_____
_____

# Greeting War

## Students will increase their vocabulary of different types of greetings.

Greeting war is similar to the card game War, in that each player goes back and forth until someone wins. In Greeting War there are two players and each player will say a greeting, without repeating, until someone can't think of one. If you are caught not being able to think of a greeting, then you lose that round. You can start fresh with the greetings each round. Whoever wins the most rounds, wins.

The instructor can start the activity by explaining in depth what a greeting is and what purpose it serves. If you need assistance you can read the sample below.

*"Greetings are how we start a conversation. They usually include the person's name and a friendly smile. They are a polite way to get someone's attention and to break the ice in an awkward silent situation. Greetings should be done by everyone participating in the conversation."*

Some examples of greetings are:
- "Hi (name), how are you?"
- Comment on the weather "It's so hot out there today"
- Hello
- Hey there
- How have you been?
- Good Morning!

# Greeting War

Make a list of as many greetings as you can think of.

# Group Ball Challenge

Students will work together to achieve a goal.

Materials:

- Inflatable ball

Students will form a circle in an open space (ex: outdoors or in a gym). The teacher will begin by discussing the rules and then introducing the challenge.

Rules of the game:

- If the ball hits the ground the group must start over.
- Keep everyone safe by respecting each other's space.
- Only respectful comments are allowed.
- (Difficult Variation) everyone must touch the ball at least once.

Challenge Ideas:

- Say a letter of the alphabet every time someone hits the ball before it hits the ground.
- Count every time some hits the ball before it hits the ground. This challenge can be made more difficult by having students practice their times table or any other easy to remember facts.

The rules are simple for a reason. This activity should be mainly run by the students with as little input from the teacher as possible. The teacher should facilitate the activity by providing and enforcing the rules and mediating the discussion of ideas if needed. Students should set a goal for themselves and periodically throughout the activity, the teacher should hold the ball and ask a few probing questions.

Questions:

- How is the group doing at achieving their goal?
- What things are working?
- What things aren't working?
- What things should be adjusted?

Let the students talk out things and make adjustments, then start again. Remember to limit your input and let the students share as many of their ideas as possible. This gives them more ownership in their achievements as a group.

**Author's note:**

*"This activity can be done throughout a school year. I did this activity with my class at the beginning of the school year and told them we would work on it throughout the year to see if we are learning how to work together better as the year goes on. We did the alphabet variation. At the beginning of the year we made it to "G" as a group. By the end of the year we made it to "T". Even though we didn't make it all the way through the alphabet my students felt accomplished and developed an appreciation for the skills needed to work together. It should be noted that my class was made up of students on the spectrum.*

# How do you think they feel?

Students will read a scenario and try to figure out how the person would feel.

Begin by talking about the meaning of empathy.

**Empathy:** the ability to understand and share the feelings of another

Use the "How do you think they feel?" worksheet to either discuss the scenarios as a group or have students individually fill out the worksheets and then talk about them together. Focus on teaching how you are able to figure out how someone else may feel from the description given. You can add some fun to the activity by reading the scenarios aloud to the class and choosing a student to act out each scenario as you read it.

Examples of how you can figure out how someone else may be feeling:

- The words being used.
- The situation being described.
- Putting yourself in the same situation and thinking about how you would feel.

# How do you think they feel?

Read the following scenarios and describe how you think the person may feel?

- Henry worked for 2 hours on his homework last night. As he walked toward the school, a car drove by a puddle and made a big splash! His clothes got a little wet but his backpack got soaked and his homework was ruined. How do you think he felt and why?

  _____
  _____
  _____

- Patrick was crying in class because his puppy ran away the night before. How do you think he felt and why?

  _____
  _____
  _____

- Samantha is a very quiet person. She always holds her hands on her ears when there is a loud noise. While she was in class, the fire alarm went off for a fire drill. Samantha began to yell and rock back and forth. Everyone was staring at her. How do you think she felt and why?

  _____
  _____
  _____

- Adam was back in class after staying home for a few days because he had been feeling sick. After lunch he didn't appear to feel very well again. He asked the teacher if he could go use the bathroom but he didn't make it in time and had an accident in his pants. Adam's face turned bright red and his eyes started to well up with tears. How do you think he felt and why?

  _____
  _____
  _____

- Frank really struggled in math class. It was really difficult for him. One day the teacher passed back the math tests and Frank had an enormous smile on his face. I looked at his paper and noticed a big A on the top of it. How do you think Frank felt and why?

  _____
  _____
  _____

# How would you feel if?

<u>Students will read a scenario and discuss how they would feel.</u>

Begin by talking about identifying emotions in yourself. Read the following paragraph to the class.

*"Identifying emotions in yourself can be harder than you might think. Often people think they are either happy or sad but there are many other emotions they may be feeling. Generally when someone feels angry they are actually feeling sad, nervous or scared but haven't realized it and have unknowingly disguised it as feeling angry. Being able to identify how you feel will help you learn how to make yourself feel better."*

Use the "How would you feel if?" worksheet to either discuss as a group or have students individually fill it out and then talk about it together. Focus on teaching how you are able to figure out how someone else may feel from the description given. You can make this activity more fun by choosing a student to act out each scenario as you read them aloud if you choose.

# How would you feel if?

Read the following scenarios and describe how you would feel if you were in that situation?

- While you were walking into school you heard some kids making jokes about you and laughing as you walked by. How would you feel if this happened to you and why?

  _____
  _____
  _____

- While playing tag at recess with your friend, you slip and fall. Everyone starts laughing but they also ask if you are ok. How would you feel if this happened to you and why?

  _____
  _____
  _____

- After lunch your stomach is just not feeling right. You tell your teacher you don't feel well and ask if you can go to the bathroom. As you are walking out of the class, you throw up all over the floor. How would you feel if this happened to you and why?

  _____
  _____
  _____

- You told a friend of yours that you have a crush on one of your classmates but not to tell anyone because it's a secret. Later that day you overhear your friend telling someone your secret. How would you feel if this happened to you and why?

  _____
  _____
  _____

- You've spent all year practicing reading because it is always been difficult for you. During the awards ceremony at the end of the year your name is called for the most improved reader. How would you feel if this happened to you and why?

  _____
  _____
  _____

# Hygiene Experiment

<u>Students will do an experiment that shows the importance of getting clean.</u>

Materials needed:

- a sink with water
- soap
- hand towels
- olive oil

Begin by talking about what hygiene is.

**Hygiene:** keeping a clean, healthy body with a clean personal appearance

Discuss why having good hygiene is important. Brainstorm a list together as a class. Some possible reasons are:

- Keeps you healthy
- Helps you smell better so people will want to be around you
- Helps your clothes last longer
- Keeps bugs away
- Keeps your teeth strong
- Helps you avoid painful trips to the dentist
- Helps avoid infections
- Helps avoid the passing of germs and getting sick

Begin the activity by having the students put a small amount (a few drops) of olive oil on their hands. Let them try to wash the oil off of their hands by only using water. Comment on how their hands are still sticky even though they've washed them. Next have them use soap to wash their hands. Explain how your body produces oil and it is necessary to use soap when you bathe to get the oil and dirt off of your body.

# I need ...

<u>Students will read a scenario and practice requesting things they need.</u>

Begin this activity by discussing the importance in knowing how to ask for things you need. Read the following:

*"Today we are going to talk about asking for things we need. This may seem like a simple skill for some but many times people will assume that others just know what they need and think they should give it to them. This can even happen with the people we know the best. There are many times we need or want things but we don't know how to ask for them. Maybe you are in class and you need a drink of water but you don't want to ask because you just had lunch and you think your teacher will say no. So instead you sit at your desk and are unable to focus on your work. If you were able to just ask your teacher for a drink of water, then you would be able to focus better. Today we are going to practice identifying what we need and then practice asking for it."*

Hand out the "I need ..." worksheet and have your students fill it out. Once everyone is done, discuss the answers together. The teacher should read the scenario and then call on students who will then say, "I need ...." and read the answer they came up with.

After you discuss the worksheet, ask you students to think of times when they have needed something but were nervous to ask for it or didn't know how to ask. Make a list together as a class.

# I need …

You have just gotten on the bus for a field trip. Your friend asks you to sit with them all the way in the back. You rush to the back of the bus to sit with your friend but as the bus starts driving you realize you aren't feeling very well. What do you need?

"I need _____"

You are in math class trying to solve a multiplication problem but you can't remember the right order to use. You are sure you are doing it wrong but you can't remember the correct way to do it. What do you need?

"I need _____"

As you are eating lunch, your drink spills all over the floor. You didn't even take a sip yet. It gets worse. As it spilled, it leaked all over your sandwich, so now it's all soggy. What do you need?

"I need _____"

You didn't sleep very well last night because there was thunder all night long and it kept waking you up. Staying awake in class is very difficult today for that reason. You know you aren't allowed to sleep while at school but there must be something you can do to help you stay awake. What do you need?

"I need _____"

You completed your homework last night but while waiting for school to start you set your backpack down, not realizing you set it in a puddle. Your homework was ruined. What do you need?

"I need _____"

As you are sitting in the lunch room you are feeling overwhelmed by the noise. Normally you can handle it, but today it is really bothering you and you can feel your insides feeling worse and worse the louder it gets. What do you need?

"I need _____"

# Ignoring Negativity

## Students will practice focusing and ignoring negative distractions.

1. Start by setting up an outlined area to work in. You can use rope or tape on the floor. Next fill that area with lots of obstacles. You can use tipped over chairs, balls, pool noodles, or anything you have laying around.

2. The object of the activity is for you to get your teammates through the area filled with obstacles while blind folded.

3. They need to start on one end and finish on the other. Since they can't see, they will be relying on their teammates to verbally guide them through, but they are not allowed to touch their partners. To add a higher level of difficulty to the activity, have the other team members try to distract the person going through the maze with wrong directions or negative (but still appropriate) comments.

4. The person going through the maze will have to focus on the people trying to help them and do their best to block out and ignore those who are trying to hold them back. Everyone needs to stand outside of the outlined work area except for the person navigating through.

Adjust the difficulty level for the individual student going through the maze to what they can handle. The difficulty level can be adjusted by the amount of obstacles in the area and the amount of people talking to the person navigating through. If you give them more than they can handle, it is likely to be unsuccessful.

Discussion questions for after the activity.

1. What about this activity was difficult?
2. What about this activity was easy?
3. Were you able to ignore negativity and achieve your goal?
4. What helped you be successful?
5. What held you back from accomplishing your goal?
6. What did you learn from this activity?

# Interrupt or Wait

Students will talk about different situation and discuss if they should interrupt or wait.

**Interrupt:** to start talking while someone else is already talking

**Wait:** to hold off on talking until the person you want to talk to is ready

Begin by talking about the definition of the words, interrupt and wait. Talk to the class about how there are different situations that require you to respond in different ways. For example, some situations are more of emergencies and would require you to interrupt someone while other situations are more of a convenience and would require you to wait until it is your turn to talk.

Have your students fill out the "Interrupt or Wait" worksheet and then as a class discuss each situation and why you would choose to interrupt or wait.

After you review the worksheet together discuss some polite ways to interrupt if you need to. Have your students come up with as many as they can before giving them suggestions.

Some sample answers are:

- Excuse me
- Sorry to interrupt but...
- Pardon me
- I see you are busy but there is an emergency!
- Help! (only in severe emergency situations)


Together as a class, brainstorm some ways you would know if someone was done talking and it was your turn to talk. Have your students come up with as many as they can before giving them suggestions.

Some sample answers are:

- They stop talking
- They don't appear to be listening to someone else who is talking
- They look at you
- They greet you
- They go back to doing something by themselves

# Interrupt or Wait

Mark each situation with an **I** if you think you should interrupt or a **W** if you think you should wait until it's your turn to talk.

_____ You need to go to the bathroom

_____ You want to go get a drink

_____ Someone is fighting in the hall

_____ You have a question about how to do your work

_____ You are bleeding

_____ You need a pencil

_____ You saw someone get hurt

_____ You can't find your book

_____ Someone said something that hurt your feelings

_____ You heard someone say a bad word

_____ You think it's time for recess

_____ You are upset about the schedule changing

_____ You want to know what to do next

_____ You want to know when it will be time for lunch

_____ You want a snack

_____ You think you are going to throw up

_____ You need to use the bathroom and it's an emergency

_____ Other kids aren't playing by the rules at recess

_____ Your computer isn't working correctly

# Jokes: Offensive vs. Not Offensive

Students will explore the differences between offensive and not offensive jokes.

Read the following to the class:

"Joking around is something most people enjoy doing however if it's taken too far, jokes can be the opposite of funny. They can become offensive and hurt other's feelings. Jokes can even be used as a form of bullying at times, so it's important to learn the difference between jokes that are OFFENSIVE and jokes that are NOT OFFENSIVE."

Discuss the meaning of the vocab words.

**Offensive Jokes:** jokes that can hurt someone's feelings or make them feel targeted

**Not Offensive Jokes:** jokes that don't attack another person's beliefs, ethnicity, gender, or anything that makes them who they are

Have you students fill out the "Offensive Jokes vs. Not Offensive Jokes" worksheet and then discuss the answers together as a class. After you feel like your students understand the difference, you can let them share their own jokes that are not offensive.

# Offensive Jokes vs. Not Offensive Jokes

Mark the line with an ☹ if you think it would be offensive and an ☺ if you think it would not be offensive.

_____  Jokes containing swear words

_____  Jokes about the chicken crossing the road

_____  Knock knock jokes

_____  Your mama jokes

_____  Jokes about people's ethnicities

_____  Jokes about someone's religion

_____  Jokes about people who have disabilities

_____  Animal jokes

_____  A clever play on words

_____  Blonde jokes

Can you think of a joke that is <u>Not Offensive</u> to share?

_____

_____

_____

_____

# Literal vs. Figurative

Students will explore the different meanings of literal and figurative phrases.

Review the necessary vocab words for this lesson.

**Literal:** something that is meant exactly as it is said
**Figurative:** something that has a different meaning than what is actually said
**Idiom:** common phrases that have figurative meanings

Have students read the phrases on the "Idioms" worksheet and discuss the real meaning of each phrase. After discussing the worksheet, try to come up with as many idioms as you can as a class or in partners and then share.

# Idioms

Write the real meaning of the common phrases listed below.

Piece of cake _____

Break a leg _____

Add fuel to the fire _____

Takes forever _____

Apple of their eye _____

Sleep on it _____

Kick yourself _____

Put your foot in your mouth _____

Wild goose chase _____

Make a beeline for it _____

Being hard headed _____

Clean as a whistle _____

A dime a dozen _____

Taste of your own medicine _____

Against the clock _____

In the same boat _____

Beat around the bush _____

Between a rock and a hard place _____

All your eggs in one basket _____

Go the extra mile _____

Icing on the cake _____

Lend me your ear _____

Turn over a new leaf _____

On the fence _____

Out of the blue _____

# Lying vs. Being Polite

Students will learn about the difference between telling a lie and being polite.

Review the necessary vocab words.

**Lying:** giving false information intentionally

**Polite:** taking someone's feelings in to consideration, using manners

After you discuss the difference between lying and being polite, have your students fill out the "Lying vs. Being Polite" worksheets and then discuss as a class.

# Lying vs. Being Polite

Read the situations described below and then write an **L** on the line if you think they are lying and a **P** on the line if you think they are being polite.

_____ You hit someone but you told your teacher you didn't, when they asked you about it.

_____ Your friend is excited to show you their new t-shirt and asks you if you like it. You say it's nice even though you wouldn't wear it.

_____ You forgot to do your homework but told your teacher you did it and someone stole it from you.

_____ You don't want to take a test so you tell your teacher you are sick and you need to call your parents.

_____ A classmate is sharing the story they wrote with the class and you don't find it to be interesting at all. When they ask you if you like it you said, "it was a good story".

_____ You were talking during class but you didn't want to get in trouble. Your teacher thought it was another student and you let them get in trouble for you.

_____ Your teacher asks you if you saw who pushed another student at recess and even though you did see them do it, you told your teacher no.

# Memory Scene

<u>Students will practice using their attention skills to figure out what changed in the scene.</u>

Begin by discussing the importance of paying attention. As a class, list some reasons why paying attention is important.

    Possible reasons:

- To know what the directions are
- To stay safe
- To know what people are expecting from you

After you have introduced the topic, begin explaining the game.

Memory Scene is a simple game where an area of a room is designated the "scene". Students will take turns being in charge of the scene.

Rules of the game:

1. The entire class will have 30 seconds to study the scene and then turn around.

2. When it is your turn to be in charge of the scene, you will change one and only one thing. (ex: move a piece of paper, or turn a stapler around)

3. The other students will then turn back around and try to figure out what changed.

4. Whoever figures out what changed first will get to go next until everyone has a turn. If someone gets it right, but has already gone, they will get to choose who goes next out of the remaining students.

# Mock Dinner Party

Students will practice table manners and requesting things they need.

Materials needed:

- Paper plates
- Paper cups
- Plastic spoons, forks and knives
- Paper napkins
- Paper to be used as placemats
- Pitcher
- Serving spoons and bowls for food that is provided
- Inexpensive food to be passed around (ex: popcorn in a bowl, fruit in a bowl)
- Inexpensive drinks in a pitcher (ex: water, juice)

1. The instructor will prepare the students for this activity by discussing table manners. Read the following:

    *"Table manners are social rules people follow while at the table. They are used to keep things sanitary (clean) and to promote being polite to others. Today we are going to have a mock dinner party. We are going to learn about table manners and how to politely request things we need or want. We will start by learning how to set the table."*

2. Group all the students together at tables or move desks together to give the appearance of a table. Make a list on the board of what each student will need.

    a. Plate

    b. Cup

    c. Napkin

    d. Plastic ware

    e. Placemat

3. Assign a student to be in charge of each object needed for a place setting and spread them out around the room. Have the other students walk around to each station and get the items they need to set their spot. In order to get an item, they must practice saying, "May I please have a _____?"

4. Once the other students have the materials they need, have the students who were assigned to handing out an objects collect their materials.

5. Provide a visual example of how to set their place setting and then walk around and help make sure they have it done. (There are different interpretations of this so use one you know or use the example provided below)

6. Once everyone has their spot set, review polite ways to request things. Have your students give examples and make a list together as a class.
   Some possible answers are:

   a. May I please have the…

   b. Can you pass the…

   c. When you're done, could I have the…

   d. Can I please have…

7. Place bowls of food and pitchers of drinks on the table. Tell your students the only way to get food or a drink is to have someone pass it to you. You may not pick something up and give it to yourself. In order to get someone to pass it to you, you must use a polite phrase to request the item you want. All requests should include "please" and then "thank you".

8. Before you begin, remind your students the **purpose of this activity is to practice requesting things they need and to practice being polite**. Part of being polite is being patient and waiting for your turn. Dinner parties are also a great time to practice conversation skills. Encourage your students to practice having conversations with the students they are seated near.

9. Once you have thoroughly discussed the objective and the rules, they may begin.

---

### Discuss Activity

After everyone has had a chance to request items and have conversations, ask your students these questions:

- What was the purpose of this activity? (to practice requesting things they need and to practice being polite)
- Who thinks they fulfilled the purpose of the activity?
- What was hard about the activity?
- What was easy about the activity?
- What things do you feel you still need to practice?
- Where are some other places you could practice these skills?

When you are done going over the activity, ask your students one more question. "Who is responsible for cleaning up your mess?" Then have everyone clean up and move things back to where they belong.

# Patient Patty

<u>Students will discuss the importance of being patient.</u>

Begin by asking your students if they know what being patient is. Review the definition of patience.

**Patience:** waiting politely for your turn or for something to happen

Read the Story, <u>Principal Helen Presents, Patient Patty</u> to the class and talk about the discussion questions at the end.

# Principal Helen Presents: **Patient Patty**

*Patty is a fourth grade student at So. Shell Elementary. She seemed to always be in a hurry. When it was time for recess, she was half way out the door before the teacher finished telling the class to line up. At lunch she would push everyone out of the way to be the first in line. She was in such a rush she didn't realized how angry she made her classmates when she would hurry past them.*

*One day in class, Mrs. Davey told her students she had some big news. She told them if they could get an A on their upcoming math test then they could earn a bonus field trip to the zoo. Patty loved going to the zoo and couldn't wait to take the math test and go! She studied every day for the test.*

*When the test day came, Patty hurried to class and eagerly sat in her seat. Mrs. Davey went over the directions with the class before handing out the test and reminded everyone to take their time and read all of the directions before answering the questions. As soon as Mrs. Davey put the test on Patty's desk, Patty hurried and put her name on the test and then began. She skimmed through the questions and saw the numbers. She knew they had been practicing multiplication in class so she quickly multiplied the numbers together and moved on to the next question and the next question and the next question. Before she knew it, she was done! She rushed to Mrs. Davey's desk to hand in her test with a smile on her face. All she could think of was the zoo!*

*The next day Mrs. Davey handed the tests back out to the students. Patty was excited to get her test. She knew how to multiply very well and had no doubt she was going to the zoo. When she looked at her test, her face went blank. She didn't get an A. She didn't even get a B. Patty saw a big D on her paper. She became very upset and had a hard time controlling herself.*

*She ran up to Mrs. Davey and started yelling, "How could I get a D?? I must go to the zoo! Why did you give me a D?"* Mrs. Davey asked Patty to calm down and quietly come talk to her, but Patty was just too mad. She continued to yell, so Mrs. Davey sent Patty to Principal Helen's office.

Patty was still very upset, but had managed to calm herself down while waiting for Principal Helen to call her into her office. Principal Helen opened her door and asked Patty to come in. Principal Helen asked her what happened. Patty broke down crying and said "I know how to multiply very well! I practiced every night! How could I get a D and not be able to go to the zoo?"

Principal Helen told Patty she was sorry she was so upset about the field trip to the zoo. She reminded Patty that even when you are upset, it's still not ok to yell at those around you. Patty felt bad and said sorry for yelling. She said she was just so upset because she knew how to multiply and she should have gotten an A on the test.

Principal Helen explained to Patty that she had spoken with Mrs. Davey and found out why her score was so low on the test. Mrs. Davey had told Principal Helen that Patty was in fact very good at multiplying, one of the best in the class, however the test was not just about multiplication." Patty's face dropped.

Principal Helen went on to say "The test also reviewed things you learned in math earlier in the year. Mrs. Davey was surprised that you did so poorly on the test as well, but explained how you tend to rush through things." Mrs. Davey suspected that Patty had rushed through the test as well. Patty admitted to rushing through the test. She said "I was just so sure I knew what I was doing."

"Principal Helen then explained to Patty that "even though we may think we know what is coming next, it is still very important to wait for directions. When we rush through things, we often miss out on a lot." Yeah, I guess you are right" said Patty. Principal Helen went on to say, "We miss out on having fun with those around us and we miss important information."

Principal Helen explained "this skill is called patience. It is a skill that needs to be practiced and can be very hard for many people, even adults." Patty replied, "You're *right. If I had practiced patience I'm sure I would have gotten an A on the test and then would be going to the zoo."* Patty thanked Principal Helen for talking with her. She had learned her lesson and would practice being more patient from then on.

Discussion Questions:

1. What would happen when Patty would rush through things?
2. Why is it important to take your time doing things?
3. Did rushing all of the time get Patty what she wanted?
4. What could Patty have done differently to be able to go to the zoo?
5. Have you ever found yourself rushing through things?
6. What has happened to you in the past when you have rushed?
7. What does patience mean?
8. Do you think you are good at being patient or is it something you have a hard time with?

# Positive and Negative Consequences

<u>Students will complete the scenarios in the chart to determine a likely outcome.</u>

Review the meaning of the necessary vocab word:

**Consequence:** the result of an action or choice that can be either positive or negative

Students will complete the "Positive and Negative Consequences" worksheet and determine a likely outcome based on their choice of response to the situations presented.

Discuss the process of behavior together with your class. If you need help, read the following:

*"Our behavior is something we are in total control of. When something undesirable happens, we have a choice. We can either choose to respond appropriately to the situation and increase our chances of a positive result or we can choose to respond negatively and likely receive a negative result. Once you understand how the behavior cycle occurs, you are more equipped to think through your choices and you will have a much better chance for positive results."*

# Behavior Cycle

| What happened to upset you? | What response did you choose? | What was the result of your choice? |
|---|---|---|
| *Ex: You accidently have your brother's lunch instead of yours and it has the wrong kind of chips.* | *Ex: You get very upset and throw your lunch away.* | *Ex: You are now hungry the rest of the day because you didn't eat anything at lunch.* |
| The teacher changed the schedule today and now you are missing your favorite class. | | |
| It started raining right before recess so now you have to stay inside. | | |
| Your car gets stuck in traffic on the way to school and you have to wait an extra hour in the car. | | |
| You want to go play in the park but you have to do homework first. | | |

# Positive Consequences

# vs.

# Negative Consequences

Students will explore the different outcomes of different choices.

Begin by discussing the meaning of consequence:

**Consequence:** the result of an action or choice that can be either positive or negative

This chart can be used to help explain the different outcomes that occur with different choices. It should not be used while the student is still upset. It can be helpful before or after an incident occurs, once the student is calm and is ready to process.

Depending on the student's level, you could have them fill it out on their own and then discuss it together or you could fill it out together with the instructor guiding them through the process. It can be filled out by drawing pictures as well.

This chart is meant to be used as a teaching tool and not a punishment.

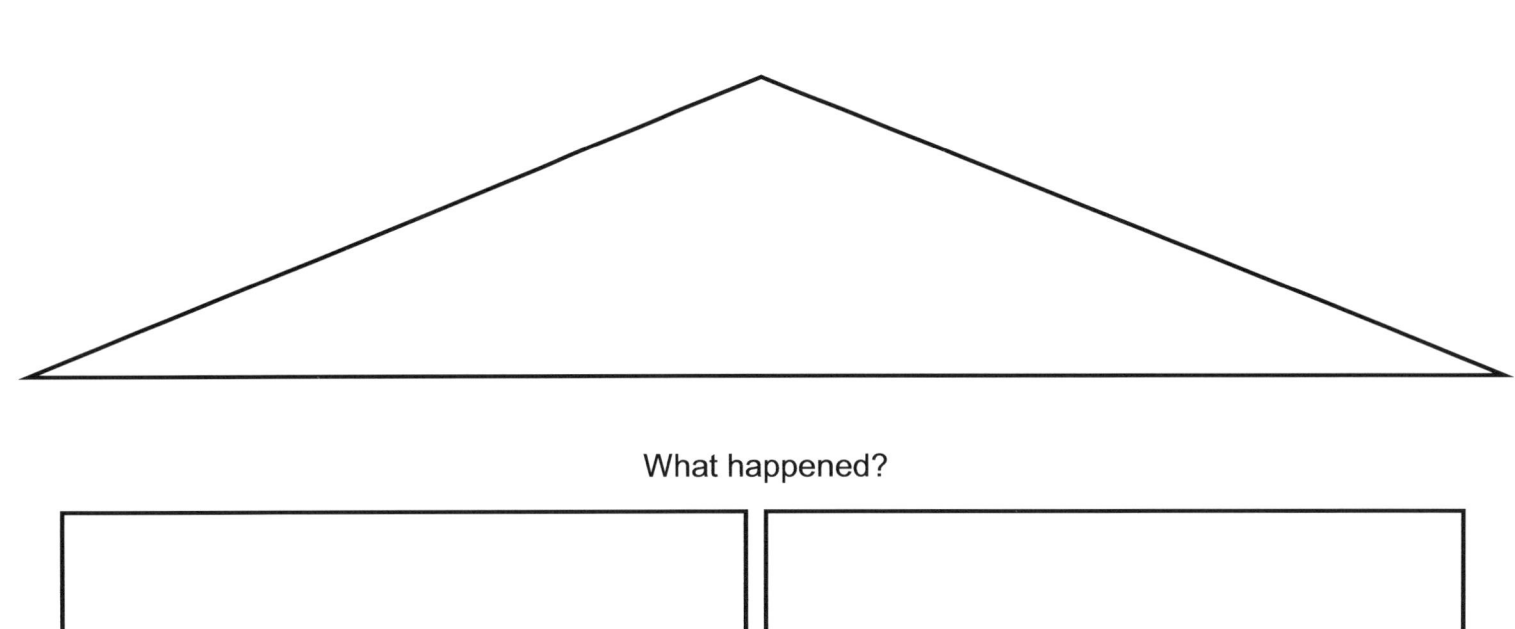

What happened?

Positive Choice                                              Negative Choice

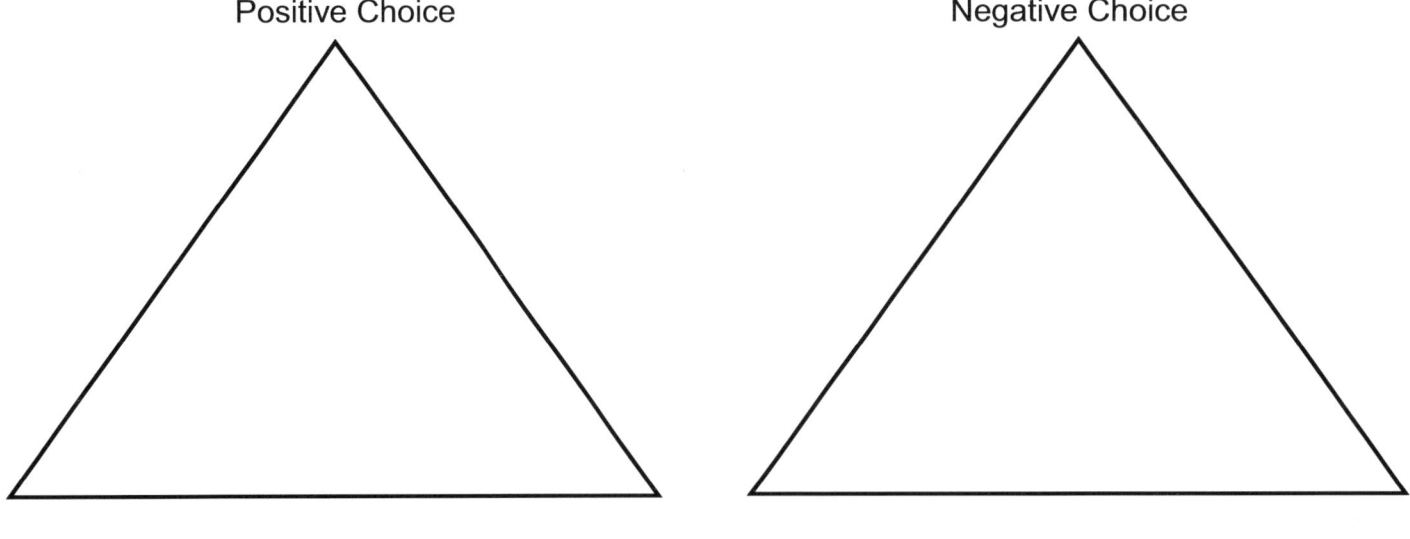

Positive Outcome                                             Negative Outcome

96

# Punctuality

<u>Students will discuss the importance of being on time.</u>

Begin by discussing the meaning of being punctual.

**Punctual:** arriving on time

Discuss how being punctual can be more important in some situation than in others but how it is good to practice being punctual all the time. Also discuss how showing up late can be interpreted as being disrespectful and disorganized.

Read the situations below and discuss what might happen if you weren't on time.

- Showing up late to a movie.
- Being late for school
- Being late for work
- Arriving to a sporting event late
- Being late when meeting your friends to play
- Arriving late to a wedding
- Being late for a doctor appointment
- Being late to a birthday party
- Arriving late to the public pool

(Continued on next page)

Discuss what some benefits to being on time are. Some possible answers are listed below.

- Get a good seat at the movie.
- Not missing any directions at school
- Keeping your job
- Watching the opening show at a sporting event
- Having more time to play with your friends
- Not being disrespectful of other people's time
- Seeing the Bride and Groom get married
- Not having to reschedule your doctor appointment
- Enjoying the entire birthday party and not missing any of the fun
- Getting a good spot at the pool
- Getting a good seat

# Punctuality

Write a possible outcome for showing up late to the following scenarios.

Showing up late to a movie

_____

Being late for school

_____

Being late for work

_____

Arriving to a sporting event late

_____

Being late when meeting your friends to play

_____

Arriving late to a wedding

_____

Being late for a doctor appointment

_____

Being late to a birthday party

_____

Arriving late to the public pool

_____

# Reading Nonverbal Social Cues

<u>Students will look for and guess the meaning of nonverbal social cues.</u>

Materials:

- Movie clip of a person with animated body language from a movie that is not familiar to your students.

Begin by discussing the meaning of nonverbal social cues:

**Nonverbal Social Cues:** information given by a person through their body language and facial expressions, rather than words being spoken

Follow the directions below:

1. The instructor should choose a clip from a movie that their students are not familiar with. The scene should include someone with animated body language. (Think of I Love Lucy types of body language).
2. Once you have a clip chosen, play it with the volume off.
3. Ask your students to watch the clip and try to figure out how the person in the scene is feeling. (this is why it's important to choose a movie they aren't familiar with)
4. After watching the scene, make a list of what the students think the character is feeling.
5. Watch the movie clip again together, only turn the volume on this time.
6. Discuss how the character was feeling and what nonverbal social cues they gave to let us know this, even when you're unable to hear what they were saying.

(Continued on next page)

Finish by asking students why it is important to pay attention to nonverbal cues and make a list of reasons together.

Some possible answers are:

- To understand how they are feeling
- To see if they are paying attention to you when you talk
- To see how they feel about what you are saying

# Reading Nonverbal Social Cues

While watching the movie clip without any volume, try to figure out how the character(s) may be feeling.

How do you think the character(s) is/are feeling?

_____

_____

_____


What nonverbal social cues did you observe to make you think they were feeling that way?

_____

_____

_____

_____

_____

_____

After watching with the volume on, were you right about how they were feeling?

_____

_____

# Recognizing Emotions

Students will practice looking at facial expressions and recognizing different emotions.

Review the meaning of the necessary vocab word.

**Nonverbal Social Cues:** information given by a person through their body language and facial expressions, rather than words being spoken

Use the "Recognizing Emotions" worksheet to have your students practice looking at facial expressions and make a guess at how they are feeling. After your students have completed the worksheet, discuss each face and what facial expressions helped you understand how they were feeling.

# Recognizing Emotions

Use the list of emotions below to label how each person may be feeling in each picture.

- Nervous
- Lonely
- Happy
- Angry
- Disappointed
- Excited
- Sad
- Serious

_____   _____

_____   _____   _____

 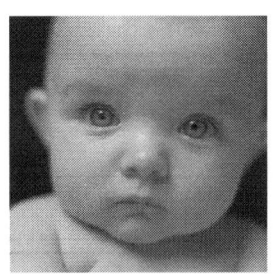 

_____   _____   _____

# Respect Form

<u>Students will use this form to help them understand the meaning of being respectful.</u>

The Respect Form can be used when you have a student who has been disrespectful, either towards people, objects or property. The questions are structured to guide them through the situation and help them understand how they were disrespectful. This is frequently used after an incident but it could also be used to prepare students before events like an assembly with a guest speaker or a field trip, where they will be in a new environment.

This form is meant to be used as a teaching tool and not a punishment.

# Respect Form

Who or what were you disrespectful to?

_____

_____

What did you do that was disrespectful?

_____

_____

_____

Who did it affect?

_____

_____

How did it affect them?

_____

_____

_____

Why do you think you made the choice you made?

_____

_____

_____

What would be a better choice to make next time?

_____

_____

_____

Did you give a sincere apology to whoever was affected?

_____

# Respectful Ryan

<u>Students will discuss respect and issues surrounding it.</u>

Review the meaning of respect with your students.

**Respect:** showing an appreciation for feelings or belongings of others

Read the Story, <u>Principal Helen Presents, Respectful Ryan</u> to the class and then talk about the discussion questions at the end.

# Principal Helen Presents: **Respectful Ryan**

*The first snow fall of the year had begun and winter break was only two weeks away. Ryan was a 5th grader who loved playing in the snow almost as much as he loved celebrating Christmas. Ryan was a very generous kid. While he enjoyed opening gifts on Christmas morning, he enjoyed doing things to help others even more. Every year he would use the money he saved throughout the year to buy toys for kids who didn't have much. Ryan was always thinking of others.*

*One day at school Ryan overheard some kids making fun of Phil. "He doesn't even have a Christmas tree!" they said, as they laughed and pointed at Phil. Ryan could tell this made Phil very uncomfortable. "Why don't you have a tree in your house?" the boys asked. "Everyone has a tree during Christmas time!" the boys exclaimed. Phil started to say, "Well.....my family doesn't celebrate Christmas. We..." and before he could finish the boys interrupted. "WHAT??!" they shouted! "You don't celebrate Christmas?!" they said again while laughing.*

*Ryan could see that the boys were making him feel bad. He knew he had to help out Phil. The boys who were teasing Phil were usually very nice boys. Ryan realized they must just not know that not everyone believes the exact same thing.*

*That evening Ryan spoke with his mom about what he heard at school and how he wanted to help Phil feel better, but didn't know what to do. His mother told him, "I'm happy you are thinking of others and want to help." His mother went on to say, "Phil's family is Jewish and celebrates Chanukah. Maybe you could learn a little about what Phil's family believes and why they don't have a tree in there house?" Ryan thought this was an excellent idea! He decided to look up Chanukah on the internet. He found a game that was popular during this time of year called the dreidel game. Just then he had a great idea!*

*He asked his mother if she could take him to the store to get some supplies with some of the money he saved. She knew Ryan was always thinking of ways to help out others so she happily agreed. They jumped in the car and headed off to the store.*

*The next day Ryan approached Phil and told him he had an idea. As he whispered his idea to Phil, a smile came across Phil's face. They approached their teacher and told her the idea. She agreed and told them after lunch they could carry out their plan.*

*The class returned to the classroom after lunch and the teacher asked Phil and Ryan to come to the front of the room. They were going to show the class how to play a Chanukah game. Phil explained a little about what Chanukah was and both Phil and Ryan taught the class the rules of the game. Ryan had bought the things needed to play the night before and passed them out to his classmates. Everyone had a lot of fun and learned something new about Phil.*

*Principal Helen heard about what Ryan did and decided to come talk to his class. She told the class, "I am so proud of you all! You put aside your differences and beliefs and learned about someone else's. That is called being Respectful. We are all very different in many ways and it's important to remember that and to show respect for others and their beliefs." Principal Helen announced over the school speaker that Phil and Ryan's class had earned the Respect Award for the week! The class cheered when they heard the announcement and were proud of their achievement.*

<u>Discussion Questions:</u>

1. What does being respectful mean?
2. What are some other topics people can have a hard time being respectful of?
3. Has anyone ever been disrespectful to you?
4. How did you feel when you weren't respected?
5. How do you think other people feel when they are being disrespected?
6. Have you ever been disrespectful to anyone else?
7. Why is it important for everyone to be respectful?

# Responsibility

<u>Students will explore the meaning of being responsible.</u>

Review the necessary vocabulary words for this lesson.

**Responsibility:** being in charge of something

**Consequence:** the result of an action or choice that can be either positive or negative

Discuss the importance of people being responsible. Read the following to the class:

*"We all count on others to be responsible. We count on the bus driver to come on time, farmers to grow food, our teachers to teach us what we need to know. It is important for everyone to do their part. If everyone chose to not be responsible than we would have a lot of ciaos around us and we would have a lot to do on our own. Learning to be responsible is important for everyone, including kids."*

Have your students fill out the "Responsibility" worksheet and then discuss their answers together as a class.

Possible answers for their responsibilities are:
- Passing in homework
- Doing homework
- Eating your lunch
- Asking for help

Possible answers for what could happen if they didn't do them are:
- Low grades
- Extra work to do
- Being hungry
- Being confused and not knowing what to do

# Responsibility

Come up with responsibilities and consequences for not completing responsibilities on the lists below.

What are some of your responsibilities?    What could happen if you didn't do them?

_____    _____

_____    _____

_____    _____

_____    _____

_____    _____

_____    _____

_____    _____

_____    _____

_____    _____

_____    _____

What are some reasons it is important for everyone to learn how to be responsible?

_____

_____

_____

_____

_____

# Self-Awareness and Self-Control

<u>Students will explore self-awareness and self-control.</u>

Review the necessary vocab words for this lesson.

**Self-Awareness:** being aware of how you feel about things
**Self-Control:** knowing what to do to calm yourself down when you become upset

This lesson is about self-discovery. Students will think about situations where they became upset and try to identify what types of things upset them. Then they will brainstorm ideas of things they have used in the past and things they can do in the future to help calm themselves down.

Have the students use the guided questionnaire to help them figure out what upsets them and what calms them down. If you put them in a page protector and let them use a dry erase marker you can use them over and over again. They can also be used for processing after an incident occurs. They may be able to identify these things without the questionnaire as well.

Have your students fill out the "Self-awareness and Self-control" worksheet. This is a personal activity but students are welcome to share if they want to. At the end of the activity, make a copy of their worksheet for your records and refer to it if and when they become upset and struggle with calming themselves down. Give the original copy to them so they can use it as well, if they don't use the one in their student workbook.

# Self-Awareness and Self-Control Questionnaire

1. Think about and describe a time when you became upset.

2. What feelings did you feel as a result of that happening?

3. What about the situation made you so mad?

4. What did you do to calm yourself down?

5. Did it work?

6. What else could you try to calm yourself down if that type of situation happens again?

# Self-Awareness and Self-Control

These are things that are likely to upset me:

These are things that are likely to calm me down:

# Showing Respect

Students will practice showing respect for other people's feelings and belongings.

Review the meaning of the word Respect:

**Respect:** showing an appreciation for feelings or belongings of others

Read the following scenarios with your students and discuss how you could have been more respectful if you were in those situations.

- You go to your friend's house to play. When you get out of the car you notice there is a paved walkway to the front door, but it is quicker to go across the yard. Since you are excited to play with your friend, you take the short path and run across the yard. How do you think your actions could have made the owner of the house feel? What would be a more respectful choice you could make?

- While playing at your friend's house, your friend's mom makes you pizza for lunch. The pizza is different from the kind you are used to having. When she asks "how is it?" you reply, "It's not the kind I'm used to so I don't want it." How do you think your response made your friend's mom feel? What would be a more respectful choice you could make?

- Your friend is telling you a story and it makes you think of something else, so you interrupt and start telling your story. How do you think your actions could have made your friend feel? What would be a more respectful choice you could make?

- A friend of yours has a book you've been wanting to read and they let you borrow it. Since it is a paperback book, you fold the cover back as you are reading it because it is easier to hold that way. As you are reading, you can't find your bookmark so you fold the corner of the page to save your spot. How do you think your choice to fold the book and its pages made your friend feel? What would be a more respectful choice you could make?

- Your teacher is explaining how to do a new type of math problem. As she is talking you decide to tell your friend about your weekend and how much fun you had. She asks you to be quiet, and you are for a few minutes, but then you continue to tell your friend more about the fun you had. How do you think your choice makes your teacher feel? What would be a more respectful choice you could make?

- You went out to eat with your friend and his parents. While you are at the table your friend is telling you a story. You are listening to the story and responding to him but you are also looking at things on your phone the whole time. How do you think your choice has made your friend feel? What would be a more respectful choice you could make?

# Social Circles

<u>Students will learn about the different relationships and categories people can fall into.</u>

Review the necessary vocab words for this lesson.

**Family:** people you are related to that you see on a regular basis

**Extended Family:** people you are related to that you see every now and then

**Friends:** people who are not related to you but you play with and trust

**Acquaintances:** people you see from time to time but you don't know very well

**Known Professionals:** people who you know while they work and who provide some type of service to you and/or your family

**Strangers:** people you pass by in a store or on the street that you don't know at all

    Have the students fill out the "Social Circles" worksheet and then discuss what they come up with together as a class.

# Social Circles

Use the vocab words to figure out which category the people listed below fit in and write that word on the line.

**Family:** People you are related to that you see on a regular basis.

**Extended Family:** People you are related to that you see every now and then.

**Friends:** People who are not related to you but you play with and trust.

**Acquaintances:** People you see from time to time but you don't know very well.

**Known Professionals:** People who you know while they are working and who provide some type of service to you and/or your family.

**Strangers:** People you pass by in a store or on the street that you don't know at all.

_____

_____ Your parents

_____ The person who works at the grocery store that you see every week

_____ Your cousins who live in another state

_____ Another person shopping at the store that you've never seen before

_____ The teacher you've seen in school but have never had as a teacher

_____ Your family doctor

_____ The kid in your class who you frequently play with

_____ The kid you live next door to that you play with

_____ Someone at the zoo that you've never talked to before

_____ Your brothers and sisters

_____ The police man at your school

_____ Your brother's friend who you have never played with

_____ Your dentist

_____ Someone you are standing in line behind that starts to talk to you at the store

_____ Your waitress at the restaurant you are eating at first the first time

_____ Your school principle

_____ Your parents' friends who you haven't talked to much besides saying "hi"

_____ The friendly librarian at the public library you are visiting for the first time

_____ The lunch lady at your school

_____ Your friend's parents whose house you visit a lot

# Social Games

<u>Students will practice learning the skills involved in playing with others.</u>

Materials:

- Several board games or card games

1. Social Games are done with everyday board games. This activity focuses on the skills involved when playing with others. The instructor supplies a variety of age appropriate games for the students to choose from. They should all be games that need two or more players. For students who need more intervention, a familiar game is suggested so they are focused on learning the skills instead of learning the rules of the game.

2. The students are encouraged to play with at least one person they don't talk to or play with a lot in general. For students needing more one on one intervention, an adult should either be one of the players or closely shadowing the student in need.

3. The instructor will discuss one of the skills targeted when playing with others and the students will focus on practicing that skill while playing. Start with one skill per lesson and build upon that once it is mastered. Adding in too many demands at once will likely be unsuccessful.

4. To introduce the targeted skill, you can lead your own discussion or follow the script below.

*"Today we will be focusing on _____. _____ is an important skill to learn when playing games because* _____.
*Some examples of how to* _____ *are* _____."

Social Skills involved in playing with others that should be targeted during this activity are:

- Including others
- Asking to join in
- Turn taking
- Explaining the rules
- Compromise on rules
- Patience
- Being a good sport
- Providing encouragement
- Small talk
- Sharing ideas
- Making decisions
- Listening to others

After your students have had a chance to play and practice the targeted skills, be sure to discuss how it went. You can lead your own discussion or follow the script below.

*"How many people remember what social skill we were practicing today? Raise your hand if you think you practiced _____. How did it go? Was it hard? Was it easy? Who remembers why it is important to know how to _____? Can anyone think of any other situations you may be in where knowing how to _____ would be helpful?"*

VARIATIONS:

Social games is easily adaptable by choosing games that are the age or developmental level of the students you are teaching. The same skills can be worked on at each age or developmental stage, just at different levels.

# Speed Socializing

## Students will practice learning the different parts of a conversation.

This is an activity where students pair up for 3-5 minutes and practice using their social skills. Begin by reading the following:

*"There are many skills involved in having a conversation with someone. If you don't know how to use the appropriate skills, you may come across as being rude or uninterested in what the other person is saying. The best way to practice and learn these skills is to have conversations. Today we are going to have a bunch of small conversations with each other. This activity is called, Speed Socializing. We will partner up and then I will give you a topic to discuss. You will have 3-5 minutes to discuss that topic together. Then I will say "stop" and you will find another partner and get a new topic. Remember to practice being polite by greeting your partners and ending your conversation before finding a new partner."*

To introduce the targeted skill, you can lead your own discussion or follow the script below.

*"The skill we will be focusing on today is _____. _____ is an important skill to learn when having a conversation because _____ _____. Some examples of how to _____ are _____."*

1. The instructor will give the students a topic to talk about then the students will have 3-5 minutes to talk to each other about that topic.
2. After the 3-5 minutes is up the instructor will tell the students to switch partners.
3. The instructor will give a new topic and the conversation practice will start again.
4. These rotations can go as long as the teacher feels they are beneficial. Generally 8-10 rotations has been shown to be beneficial.

Some of the skills they will focus on and practice are:

- Greetings
- Turn taking
- Staying on topic
- Showing they are listening when the other person is talking
- Showing interest in what the other person is saying
- Appropriate eye contact
- Body language
- Appropriately ending the conversation
- Politely changing the subject
- Responding politely to a rude comment
- Responding appropriately to a sensitive topic

Students should focus on working on one new targeted each time you do this lesson while building on the previous skills you've learned.

VARIATIONS:

This activity can be adapted to different age and developmental stages by choosing topics that are appropriate for that group. Some suggested topics are:

| Low | Medium | High |
| --- | --- | --- |
| Pets ( had, have, want) | Pets ( had, have, want) | Pets ( had, have, want) |
| Favorite thing to do | Favorite Hobby or pass time | What is a hobby you have never done but would like to try? |
| Favorite thing to do at recess | Favorite things to do after school that includes other people | Favorite thing to do with your friends |
| Vacations (where you've been, where you would want to go) | Vacations (where you've been, where you would want to go) | Vacations (where you've been, where you would want to go, who you would want to go with you) |
| Musical Instruments (you have tried playing or want to play) | Musical Instruments (you have tried playing or want to play) | If you could be a musician what kind would you be? |
| Favorite movies/shows | Favorite movies | If you could be in a movie, what movie would you want to be in. |
| Favorite Holiday | Favorite Holiday and why | Holiday traditions in your family |
| Favorite books | Favorite books | If you wrote a book, what kind of book would you write? |
| Favorite subject in school | Subjects that interest you to learn about | What you want to do for a job |
| Favorite thing to have for lunch | Favorite meal or restaurant | Cooking (what you can cook well, what you would like to cook) |

# Spoons

<u>Students will play a game that requires them to pay attention to win.</u>

Materials:

- A deck of cards for every 6-8 students
- Plastic spoons (enough for each student to have 1)

Review the necessary vocab word.

**Attention:** where a person's focus and interest is directed

Prepare your students by explaining you will be practicing your attention skills today. Read the following.

*"Paying attention is an important skill to have when interacting with others. If you are unable to pay attention, then you will likely miss a lot of important information. Today we will practice paying attention to what is going on around us by playing a card game. The object of the game is to grab a spoon and stay in the game. There are two ways you can grab a spoon. Either by getting all 4 of the same cards or by paying attention and seeing when someone else grabs a spoon."*

# Spoons

The rules of the game are:

1. The students will sit in a circle with one less spoon than students in the middle of the circle. (If you have 8 students in the circle you would have 7 spoons)
2. A full deck of cards will be shuffled and handed out. Each player in a group gets 4 cards to keep to themselves.
3. The object of the game is to get all of the same type of card (4 queens, 4 aces, etc.)
4. To play the game, the remaining amount of cards will be placed face down in a pile and the first person to go will grab the top card. Depending on what it is, they will either replace one of their 4 cards with it and pass on the card being replaced or pass on the card they drew.
5. The entire circle will eventually be going all at the same time. So everyone will be distracted.
6. If anyone gets all of the same 4 cards then they will grab a spoon. Be sure to grab the spoon as inconspicuously as possible. Continue to pass cards along with the group.
7. Once another player notices someone had picked up a spoon, they can also pick up a spoon. Again, as inconspicuously as possible.
8. Once all of the spoons are picked up, the last person without a spoon is out.
9. The game starts again with one less spoon.
10. The game continues until only one person is left. That person is the winner!

# Spotting Danger

<u>Students will look at a scene and spot what's dangerous, then brainstorm alternative choices.</u>

Review the necessary vocab word for this lesson.

**Danger:** possible risk of getting hurt

Introduce this lesson by talking about danger. Read the following:

*"Danger can be where we least expect it. While it's not healthy to walk around fearing everything, it is wise to be aware of your surroundings so you can make safe choices. Making safe choices won't guarantee you will never get hurt but it will surely increase your chances of staying safe."*

Have your students look at the "Spotting Danger" worksheet. Depending on their academic level, either look at each scene and talk about them together or have them fill it out on their own first and then discuss their answers together.

# Spotting Danger

Look closely at the scenes below and describe what is dangerous about them. Then come up with a safe choice you could make if you were in that situation.

What is dangerous about this scene? _____
_____

What would be a safe choice? _____
_____
_____

What is dangerous about this scene? _____
_____

What would be a safe choice? _____
_____
_____

What is dangerous about this scene? _____
_____

What would be a safe choice? _____
_____
_____

What is dangerous about this scene? _____

_____

What would be a safe choice? _____

_____

_____

What is dangerous about this scene? _____

_____

What would be a safe choice? _____

_____

_____

What is dangerous about this scene? _____

_____

What would be a safe choice? _____

_____

_____

What is dangerous about this scene? _____

_____

What would be a safe choice? _____

_____

_____

# Taking Turns in a Conversation

Students will practice waiting their turn to talk when in a conversation.

Begin by reviewing the necessary vocab words for this lesson.

**Turn Taking:** sharing an interaction with others

**Patience:** waiting politely for your turn or for something to happen

Follow the list below to lead the activity.

1. The instructor will have the students gather in a circle and tell them they are going to practice taking turns while talking.
2. The instructor will lead a discussion in why it is important to take turns while talking to someone.
3. Have the students brainstorm some reasons why it is important and make a list together.

Some possible answers are:

- To hear what each person is saying
- Being polite
- Being respectful

4. Choose an object to use as the microphone. You can use something that looks like a microphone or something silly that will entertain and keep the student's interest. It just has to be something they can toss around without hurting anyone.
5. Once you have your object, tell your students the rules of the game.

The rules are:

- You can only talk when you have the object.
- Your comments must be relevant to the subject being discussed.
- The person with the object gets to pick the next person that gets to talk by tossing them the object.
- Only toss the object to people who are paying attention.

6. When everyone knows the rules, you may begin. The instructor will introduce the subject. Try to think of topics that interest your students and that they are knowledgeable about. Encourage your students to stay on topic.

Some sample topics are:

- Favorite things to eat
- Favorite things to do over summer break
- Pets
- Movies and books
- Favorite subjects in school
- Hobbies
- Things that are challenging
- Things that are easy
- Places they would like to go
- Superhero powers they would like to have
- Things they would like to change

# Things in Common Circle

Students will get to know more about people they have things in common with.

Introduce this activity by talking about having things in common.

Read the following:

*"Many times people will develop friendships with those they have things in common with. It helps to know what you have in common with others because it can give you a topic to discuss that you are both interested in. Today we are going to play a game that highlights the things we have in common with others."*

How the game works:

1. Have your students make a circle. Everyone needs to stand relatively close to each other in the circle. (you can make an X on the floor with tape for each spot a person should be standing in, if necessary) The instructor will start in the middle.

2. The person in the middle will say something they've done before (ex: anyone who has ridden a horse).

3. Then everyone in the circle who has done the thing said by the person in the middle (ex: ridden a horse) before will have to find a different spot in the circle and the instructor will take one of their spots. (similar to musical chairs only no one gets out)

4. The person who is last to find a spot will be in the middle of the circle and then it is there turn to say something they've done (ex: anyone who has flown in a plane).

5. The game continues like this until the teacher feels everyone has moved around positions and had a chance to participate.

After you have played the game, review the activity by asking these questions to your students:

- What do you think the purpose of this game was?
- How many people learned new things about their classmates?
- Was there anyone you found out you had more in common with than you thought?
- Did you learn anything interesting about anyone else?

# Things in Common Circle

What do you think the purpose of this game was?

_____
_____

How many people learned new things about their classmates?

_____
_____

Was there anyone you found out you had more in common with than you thought?

_____
_____

Did you learn anything interesting about anyone else?

_____
_____

List some people you have things in common with and what you have in common.

_____
_____
_____
_____
_____

# Tone of Voice Game

<u>Students will practice using and identify feelings through tone of voice.</u>

Begin by discussing the necessary vocab word for this lesson. Then read the following statement.

**Tone of Voice:** the level of volume and emotion used when saying words

*"The tone of voice someone uses plays a big part in delivering a message. You can tell a lot about how someone is feeling simply by the tone of their voice. Tone of voice can be the difference between a genuine statement and a sarcastic one. We are going to play a game that lets us practice recognizing and practice using different tones of voice and see how our tone of voice changes what we are saying."*

- This is a variation of the game charades, although in this version talking is allowed. Students will try to guess the mood of the person going, simply by the tone of voice they use.
- Students will start by drawing a "tone of voice" card as well as a "statement" card. Most likely the tone of voice and statement won't match up and will sound funny together. This is to help emphasize the tone of voice being used. It's important for the students guessing to focus on the tone of voice being used and not what is being said.
- Whoever guesses correctly gets to go next until everyone has taken a turn. If someone guesses correctly but has already gone, then they can choose someone who hasn't gone yet to go in their place.

**Tone of Voice Cards**

| Tired | Excited | Annoyed |
|---|---|---|
| Interested | Bored | Happy |
| Sad | Nervous | Cranky |

**Statement Cards**

| I am going camping this weekend. | I have math class after lunch. | I have pizza for lunch today. |
|---|---|---|
| My bedtime is 9 pm. | My birthday is next week. | I am riding the bus to school tomorrow. |
| We have a field trip next week. | I have a lot of homework tonight. | My family is going to a restaurant tonight. |

# What could happen if?

<u>Students will discuss the possible outcomes of having bad hygiene.</u>

Begin by talking about what hygiene is.

**Hygiene:** keeping a clean, healthy body with a clean personal appearance.

    Once your students have a basic understanding of what hygiene means, use the "What could happen if?" worksheet. Use this worksheet to either discuss topics as a group or have students individually fill out the worksheet and then talk about their answers together.

Some possible answers when talking about the worksheet are:

- You could need a lot of dental work
- You may smell
- People may not want to be around you
- You could get sick
- You may become a target for bullies
- You may look gross to others

# What could happen if?

Answer the questions by trying to think about what could happen in each scenario.

- What could happen if you don't brush your teeth?

  _____
  _____

- What could happen if you wear your clothes while they are dirty?

  _____
  _____

- What could happen if you don't wash your hands?

  _____
  _____

- What could happen if you don't wash your hair regularly?

  _____
  _____

- What could happen if you don't shower or bathe regularly?

  _____
  _____

- What could happen if you wear your tennis shoes without socks?

  _____

  _____

- What could happen if you don't wear deodorant?

  _____

  _____

- What could happen if you don't brush your hair?

  _____

  _____

- What could happen if you wear your coat all day long while you are inside?

  _____

  _____

- What could happen if you have bad hygiene?

  _____

  _____

# What I like about you

## Students will practice giving compliments to others.

Review the necessary vocab word for this activity.

**Compliment:** recognizing and expressing something positive about someone else

This is an activity that is great for building self-esteem. Begin by discussing the purpose of a compliment by reading the following:

*"A compliment is when someone recognizes and expresses something positive about someone else. It should be individualized, meaning it should have to do with that specific person. Compliments usually make people feel good about themselves and when people feel good about themselves they are more likely to give compliments to others as well."*

How the Activity works:

1. Your students will each receive the "What I like about you" worksheet. They will spend a few minutes decorating the center circle making sure to include their name in it.

2. The instructor will designate a pattern to pass the paper in (ex: everyone pass to the person on their right).

3. Once everyone has written their name and decorated their spot on the paper they will begin a passing train.

4. When you receive someone else's paper, you will write something you like about that person in one of the spaces and then pass the paper on.

5. This will continue until everyone has written on everyone else's paper. At the end each student will have a paper full of compliments about them.

After all the sheets have been filled out and returned, the teacher will ask the class questions to review the activity:

1. How did it make you feel when you read the comments on your sheet?

2. How did you feel when you were writing compliments about other people?

3. What do you think would happen if people spent more time complimenting others?

# What I like about You!

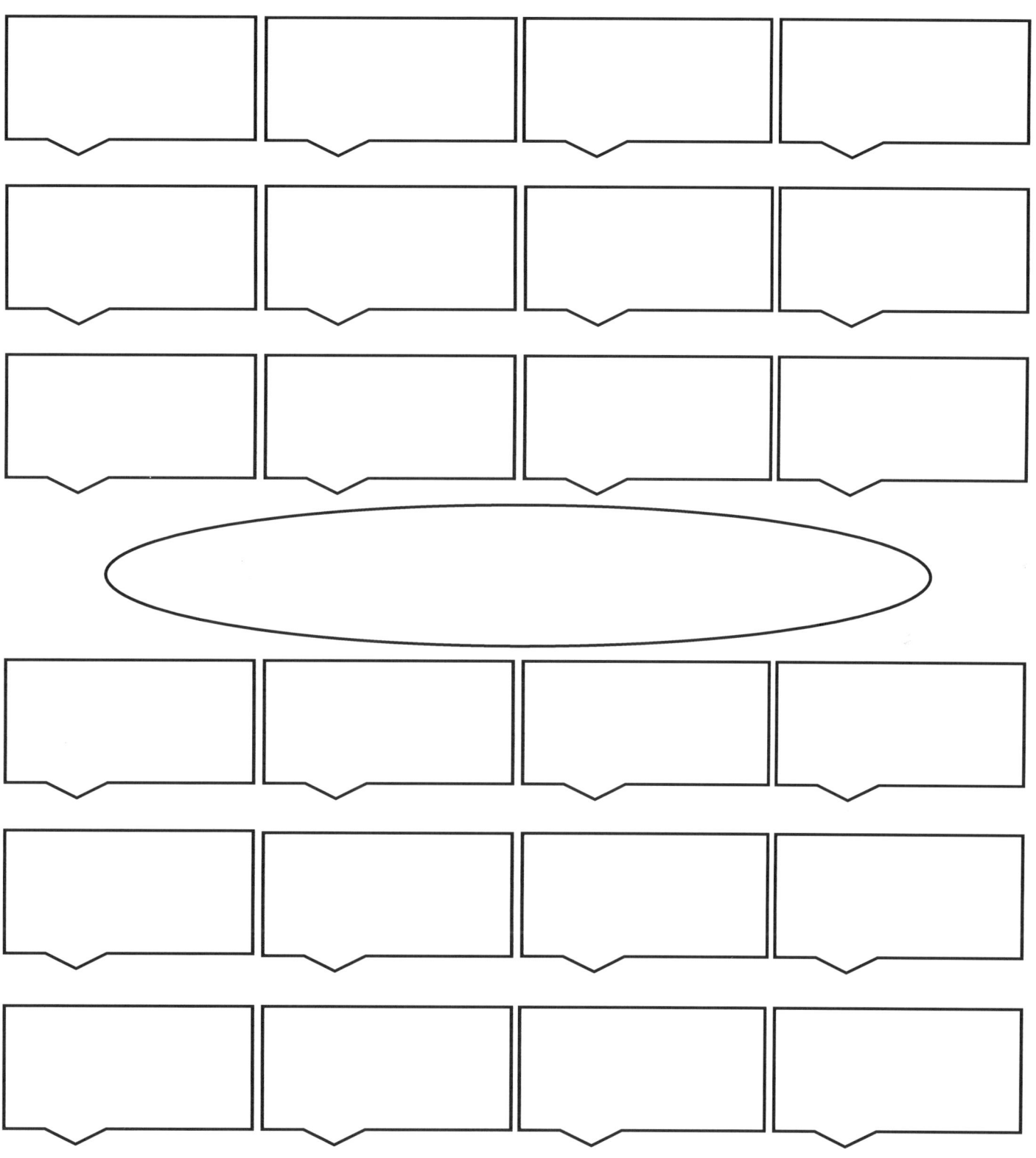

# What information is safe to share?

<u>Students will take a quiz and discuss what they should and shouldn't share with others.</u>

Set up this activity by discussing the difference between: Family, Friends, Known Professionals, Acquaintances, and Strangers.

**Family:** people you are related to that you see on a regular basis

**Friends:** people who are not related to you but you play with and trust

**Known Professionals:** people who you know while they are working and who provide some type of service to you and/or your family (doctors, teachers, police, etc...)

**Acquaintances:** people you see from time to time but you don't know very well (mailman, store worker, etc.)

**Strangers:** people you pass by in a store or on the street that you don't know at all

After you discuss the different types of people in your life, do the following:

1. Have your students fill out the "What Information is Safe to Share?" worksheet.

2. After everyone has filled out the worksheet, discuss each topic together as a class.

3. Talk about the danger of sharing the wrong information with the wrong people.

4. Talk about who it is safe to share each topic with.

5. Discuss what to do if someone shares information with you that they shouldn't share.

# What information is safe to share?

Circle all of the types of people the information listed would be safe to share with.

- Who is it safe to share your name with?
    Family    Friends    Known Professionals    Acquaintances    Strangers

- Who is it safe to share your birthday with?
    Family    Friends    Known Professionals    Acquaintances    Strangers

- Who is it safe to share your address with?
    Family    Friends    Known Professionals    Acquaintances    Strangers

- Who is it safe to share your phone number with?
    Family    Friends    Known Professionals    Acquaintances    Strangers

- Who is it safe to share your passwords with?
    Family    Friends    Known Professionals    Acquaintances    Strangers

- Who is it safe to share your secrets with?
    Family    Friends    Known Professionals    Acquaintances    Strangers

- Who is it safe to share your family information with?
    Family    Friends    Known Professionals    Acquaintances    Strangers

- Who is it safe to share your embarrassing stories with?
    Family    Friends    Known Professionals    Acquaintances    Strangers

- Who is it safe to share your health concerns with?
    Family    Friends    Known Professionals    Acquaintances    Strangers

- Who is it safe to share your fears with?
    Family    Friends    Known Professionals    Acquaintances    Strangers

# Who to approach when you need help

Students will learn about how to tell if someone is safe to ask for help.

Review the vocab words necessary for this lesson.

**Safe:** free from harm

**Unsafe:** could cause you harm

Read the following to your class:

*"You never know where you will be when you need help. It isn't always easy to know who is safe to ask. Let's talk about some ways we can tell if someone is safe to approach or not."*

Have the class brainstorm some "safe" qualities a person could have that would make you feel safer approaching them if you needed help. Emphasize that just because a stranger is being nice doesn't mean they are safe to approach for help.

Some possible answers are:

- They are someone you know and trust
- They are a known professional in uniform
- They are family
- They are friends

Have your students fill out the "Who to approach when you need help" worksheet. Once they are done, discuss the answers and how they would know that person would be a safer choice than someone they don't know.

# Who to approach when you need help

Some people are safer to approach than others when you are in need of help. Write if you think the people described below are **SAFE** or **UNSAFE** to approach when you need help.

| | |
|---|---|
| _____ | A police officer in uniform |
| _____ | A person you've never seen before walking down the street |
| _____ | A person at the customer service desk at a store who is in uniform |
| _____ | A fire fighter in uniform |
| _____ | A close friend of your parents who you've seen your parents visit with many times |
| _____ | Someone you've seen working in your school everyday |
| _____ | A construction worker who is working in your school for a few days |
| _____ | A person who tells you they are a police officer but is not in uniform |
| _____ | One of your friend's parents whose house you've visited before |
| _____ | The person behind you in line at the store |
| _____ | A doctor or nurse in uniform at the hospital |
| _____ | A doctor or nurse in uniform at the store |
| _____ | The principle of your school |
| _____ | Your classroom teacher |
| _____ | A close friend of yours |
| _____ | A kid in your class who is mean to you sometimes |

# Whose job is it?

Students will identify their role in daily activities and situations.

Begin by discussing what accountability is.

**Accountability:** showing responsibility for your choices

Use the "Accountability Roles" worksheet and either discuss as a group or have students individually fill them out and then talk about their answers together. Take time to emphasize how even though we rely on others to help us, we are still accountable for ourselves and our choices. Try to spend time talking about each situation thoroughly. If you have time, ask your students if they have any examples of times they blamed things on others when it was really their responsibility. Ask them to elaborate and talk about whose job it really was.

# Accountability Roles

- You are going on a field trip and need your permission slip signed by your parents. You gave it to them last week and talked to them about the field trip. They commented on how it sounds like it will be fun but they still haven't signed it. Whose job is it to make sure they remember to sign it?
  _____
  _____

- You forgot to brush your teeth when you woke this morning. Your mom usually reminds you but she didn't today. Another student makes a comment about food in your teeth and you feel embarrassed. You instantly get angry at your mom for forgetting to remind you. Whose job is it make sure you brush your teeth in the morning?
  _____
  _____

- You keep forgetting to pass in your homework so your grade is lower than usual. Your parents ask you about why your grade is so low and you tell them your teacher keeps forgetting to remind you to pass in your homework. Whose job is it to make sure you pass in your homework?
  _____
  _____

- Your teacher overhears you and some of your friends using bad words at recess. When your teacher talks to you about it, you say you only did it because your friends were doing it. Should you get in trouble for using bad words or only your friends? Whose job is it to make sure you make good choices about the words you use?
  _____
  _____

- You spent too much time watching TV one night and you didn't finish your chores, so your parents took away your TV privileges for a night. You get angry at your parents because you think they should have reminded you to do you chores and you think it's not fair. Whose job is it to make sure you get your chores done?
  _____
  _____

# Generalization / Practice Ideas

**Standing up to a Bully:** The teacher will put on a "bully hat" and walk around the room saying or doing things a bully might do. The students will practice using one of the strategies they've learned to deal with bullies. Of course, the teacher is only acting and needs to make sure their students realize that.

**Polite Practice:** Students will have a daily assignment of holding the door for the person behind them when entering or exiting the building as a class (ex: going to recess). They will also practice saying "thank you" to the person who held the door for them.

**Yes/No Polite Response:** Whenever there is a class snack, students will practice saying either, "yes, please" or "no, thank you" to whoever is passing it out.

**Greeting Practice:** Students will be required to use a greeting to greet at least (# determined by teacher) of students as they enter the class at the beginning of the day.

**Ending Practice:** Students will be required to use an ending (bye, see you tomorrow, etc.) to at least (# determined by teacher) of students as they leave the class at the end of the day.

**Empathy Practice:** Before students go out to recess, ask them to observe one other person out there. They are to observe how that person is feeling and why they are feeling that way. Everyone will report on what they saw quickly when they come back inside.

**Emotional Control Practice:** Students will use the Emotional Control worksheet to identify at least 3 things that help calm them down when they are upset. Write these items down and tape them to the students' desks so it is easy to refer to if they become upset.

**Respecting People:** Students will choose an adult in the school that is not in their classroom. They will talk to that person and find out what they do at the school and then report to the class about what that person does to help the school.

**Respecting Objects/Property:** Students will choose an object at the school and identify how that object improves the quality of the school and why people should be respectful of it.

**Practice Asking for Help:** Refer to Cooperation Chain activity on page 31.

**Punctuality:** Students who are on time for class will be eligible for an incentive such as: being entered into a drawing for a prize, eligible for less work due, able to know a secret password that will be asked at the end of class for extra bonus points, etc.)

**Getting to Know Others:** Students will interview students from another class or at recess. They can make up their own question or use the ones on page 54.

**Inviting Others to Play:** Students will be challenged to invite others to play with them while at recess.

**Practice Conversation Skills:** Refer to the Speed Socializing activity on page 114.

**Practice Compromising and Turn Taking Skills:** Refer to the Social Games activity on page 112 and A Tall Order on page 5.

**Practice Being Polite and Asking for Help:** Refer to the Mock Dinner Party activity on page 79.

**Practice Encouraging Others and Working Together:** Refer to the Group Ball Challenge activity on page 60.

**Practice Cooperation and Working with Others:** Refer to the Cooperation Chain activity on page 31 and A Tall Order on page 5.

# Glossary

**Accepting others:** appreciating someone for who they are and not trying to change them or make fun of them for being different from you

**Accountability:** showing responsibility and ownership for your choices

**Acquaintances:** people you see from time to time but you don't know very well

**Attention:** where a person's focus and interest is directed

**Bored:** not being interested in what is happening around you

**Bully:** a person who tries to intimidate or mistreat someone they interpret to be weaker than them

**Compliment:** recognizing and expressing something positive about someone else

**Compromise:** when two sides give in a little and meet in the middle

**Consequence:** the result of an action or choice that can be either positive or negative

**Coping:** appropriately dealing with a difficult feeling

**Danger:** possible risk of getting hurt

**Turn Taking:** sharing an interaction with others

**Empathy:** the ability to understand and share the feelings of another

**Expected:** things you can predict happening

**Extended Family:** people you are related to that you see every now and then

**Family:** people you are related to that you see on a regular basis

**Figurative:** something that has a different meaning than what is actually said

**Friends:** people who are not related to you but you play with and trust

**Good Sport:** a person who is able to win or lose without putting others down

**Hygiene:** keeping a clean, healthy body with a clean personal appearance

**Idiom:** common phrases that have figurative meanings

**Interrupt:** to start talking while someone else is already talking

**Known Professionals:** people who you know while they are working and who provide some type of service to you and/or your family

**Literal:** something that is meant exactly as it is said

**Lying:** giving false information intentionally

**Nonverbal Social Cues:** information given by a person through their body language and facial expressions, rather than words being spoken

**Not Offensive Jokes:** jokes that don't attack another person's beliefs, ethnicity, gender, or anything that makes them who they are

**Offensive Jokes:** jokes that can hurt someone's feelings or make them feel targeted

**Patience:** waiting politely for your turn or for something to happen

**Polite:** taking someone's feelings in to consideration, using manners

**Punctual:** arriving on time

**Respect:** showing an appreciation for feelings or belongings of others

**Responsibility:** being in charge of something

**Safe:** being free from harm

**Self-Awareness:** being aware of how you feel about things

**Self-Control:** knowing what to do to calm yourself down when you become upset

**Strangers:** people you pass by in a store or on the street that you don't know at all

**Stress:** strain that can be felt mentally, emotionally or physically

**Tone of Voice:** the level of volume and emotion used when saying words

**Unexpected:** things you can't predict happening

**Unsafe:** could cause you harm

**Wait:** to hold off on talking until the person you want to talk to is done talking

# Behavior Processing Forms

- Accountability Form
- Apology Note
- Behavior Choices and Outcomes Chart
- First Time Asked
- Respect Form
- Safety Form
- Self-Awareness / Self-Control

These forms can be used to process after an incident has occurred and once the student has calmed down. The students can either fill them out themselves, with the instructor or the instructor could use them as a guideline to draw a social story. They can also be used to help prepare a student for an anticipated difficult time as well. They are meant to be used as teaching tools and not punishments.

# Accountability Processing Form

What happened?

_____
_____
_____
_____

What role did you play in what happened?

_____
_____
_____
_____

Who was affected?

_____
_____

How do you think it made them feel?

_____
_____

How do you feel about what happened?

_____
_____

What should you do differently next time?

_____
_____
_____
_____

Dear _____

I'm _____ for _____

_____

I imagine it must have made you feel _____. Next time I will

_____

_____

                                                    _____

---

Dear _____

I'm _____ for _____

_____

I imagine it must have made you feel _____. Next time I will

_____

_____

                                                    _____

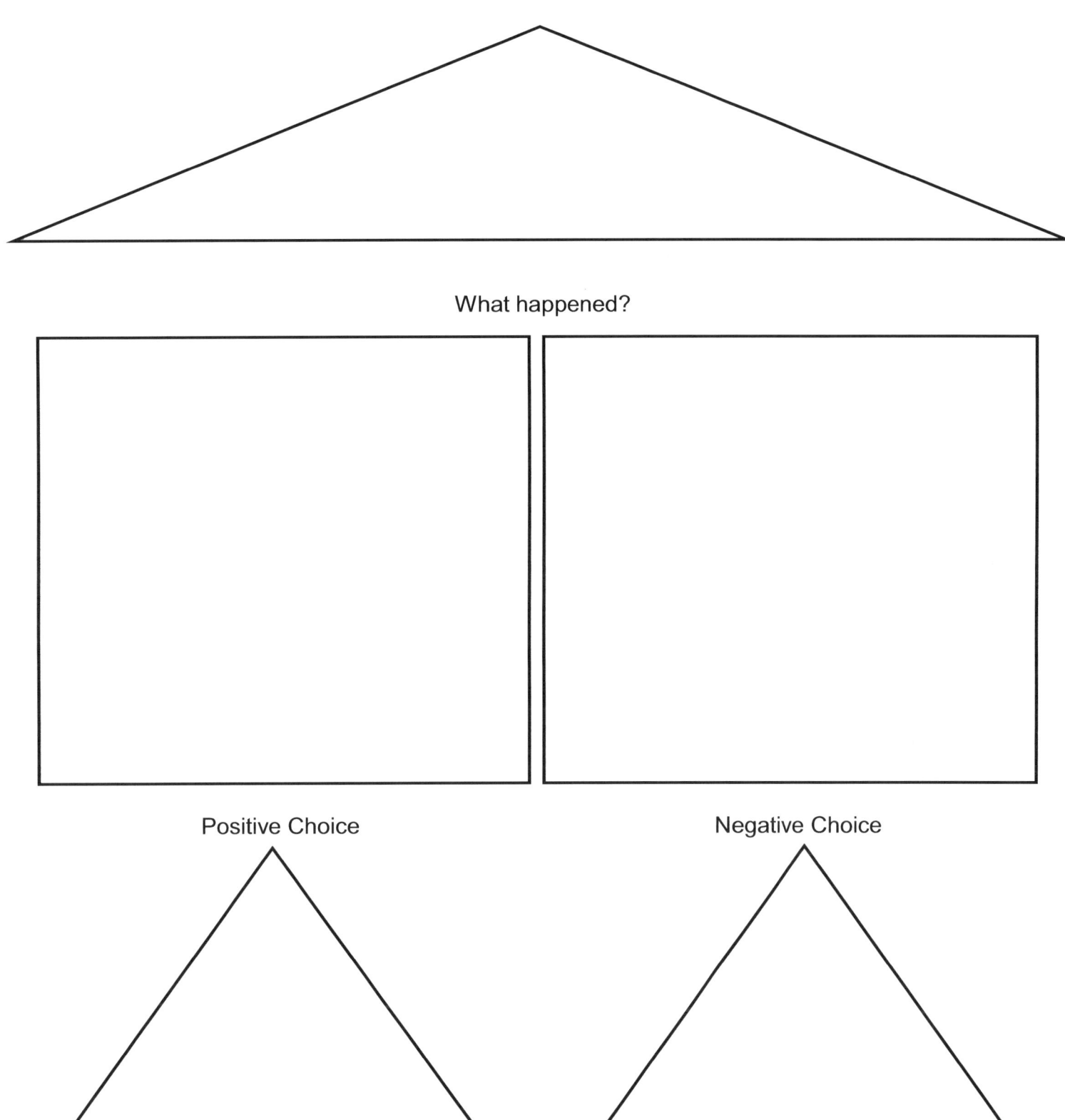

# First Time Asked

What direction did you not follow the first time?

_____
_____

Why didn't you follow the direction the first time it was given?

_____
_____

What did you do instead of following directions?

_____
_____

Who did it affect?

_____
_____

How did it affect them?

_____
_____

What should you have done?

_____
_____

Why is it important to follow directions?

_____
_____

# Respect Form

Who or what were you disrespectful to?

_____

_____

What did you do that was disrespectful?

_____

_____

_____

Who did it affect?

_____

_____

How did it affect them?

_____

_____

_____

Why do you think you made the choice you made?

_____

_____

_____

What would be a better choice to make next time?

_____

_____

_____

Did you give a sincere apology to whoever was affected?

_____

# Safety Form

**Safe:** being free from harm

Copy the definition of Safe: _____

Describe what happened to make an unsafe environment.

_____
_____
_____
_____

Whose safety did you jeopardize?

_____
_____

How did my choices make them feel?

_____
_____

What should I have done instead?

_____
_____
_____
_____

Why is it important for everyone to be safe?

_____
_____
_____
_____

# Self-Awareness and Self-Control Questionnaire

1. What happened to make you become upset?

2. What feelings did you feel as a result of that happening?

3. What about the situation made you so upset?

4. What did you do to calm yourself down?

5. Did it work?

6. What else could you try to calm yourself down if that type of situation happens again?

# How to Use the Student Social Skill Assessment

This assessment is designed to be used as a way to track data as well as determine the areas of social need for development. There are boxes located next to the date given section where you record the date you completed the assessment. Give the assessment 5 times throughout the year. A pre-assessment at the beginning of the school year, and then an assessment at the end of each term to measure for gains. Color these boxes in a different color each time you complete the assessment and use that color to fill in newly mastered skills. This will make it easier to identify when the student has mastered a skill.

The questions are written so they can easily be used as a goal on an IEP. Once you have identified the areas of need, you can use the Targeted Skills and Supporting Activities Chart on page 8 to choose the appropriate activities for the skill areas showing a deficit.

**Sample of how to fill in chart:**

No Mastery

Minimal Mastery (25%)

Moderate Mastery (50%)

Majority of Mastery (75%)

Mastered Skill (100%)

Student Name: _____

Date Given: ☐ _____ ☐ _____ ☐ _____ ☐ _____ ☐ _____

Assessment Administrators: _____

*Please color in the box next to the skills the student has mastered with the color corresponding to the date given. Be sure to use a different color each time you administer the test.*

## Accountability:

☐☐☐☐ Student is able to discuss mishaps without making excuses in 4/5 opportunities.

☐☐☐☐ Student is able to show accountability for actions without blaming others in 4/5 opportunities.

☐☐☐☐ Student is able to apologize independently and sincerely when in the wrong in 4/5 opportunities.

☐☐☐☐ Student accepts consequences without arguing in 4/5 opportunities.

## Attention:

☐☐☐☐ Student is able to show attentive listening when someone else is talking with 1 or fewer prompts in 4/5 opportunities.

☐☐☐☐ Student is able to hear and follow directions given by the teacher the first time asked in 4/5 opportunities.

☐☐☐☐ Student is able to follow directions when they are given with 1 or fewer prompts in 4/5 opportunities.

☐☐☐☐ Student is able to complete assignments within the given time period in 4/5 opportunities.

## Bullying:

☐☐☐☐ Student is able to interact with others without having complaints made about them picking on others in 4/5 opportunities.

☐☐☐☐ Student is able to express feelings appropriately when they are upset in 4/5 opportunities.

☐☐☐☐ Student interacts appropriately and appears to experience enjoyment when engaged with peers in 4/5 opportunities.

☐☐☐☐ Student is able to appropriately handle peer situations when a conflict arises in 4/5 opportunities.

## Nonverbal Communication:

☐☐☐☐ Student can make a logical assumption of how someone else is feeling based on his or her body language in 4/5 opportunities.

☐☐☐☐ Student demonstrates an understanding of what others are requesting from them in nonverbal situations (ex: holding hand up for 5) in 4/5 opportunities.

☐☐☐☐ Student displays appropriate body language while having conversations with others in 4/5 opportunities.

☐☐☐☐ Student uses an appropriate amount of eye contact when interacting with others in 4/5 opportunities.

## Verbal Communication:

☐☐☐☐ Student is able to appropriately initiate a conversation with a peer in 4/5 opportunities.

☐☐☐☐ Student takes initiative to ask questions when they don't understand something in 4/5 opportunities.

☐☐☐☐ Student responds to questions with more than one or two words in 4/5 opportunities.

☐☐☐☐ Student chooses to have conversations with others a majority of the time in 4/5 opportunities.

## Compromising:

☐☐☐☐ Student choses to play games and work with others in 4/5 opportunities.

☐☐☐☐ Student is able to appropriately disagree with someone without it turning into an argument in 4/5 opportunities.

☐☐☐☐ Student is able to successfully contribute and complete group assignments in 4/5 opportunities.

☐☐☐☐ Student is able to share ideas appropriately without quitting in 4/5 opportunities.

## Understanding Emotions:

☐☐☐☐ Student shows concern for others when they are upset in 4/5 opportunities.

☐☐☐☐ Student is able to regulate their emotions when stress occurs without blowing up in 4/5 opportunities.

☐☐☐☐ Student shows empathy for others by acknowledging how they feel in 4/5 opportunities.

☐☐☐☐ Student is able to identify how they are feeling at various times throughout the day in 4/5 opportunities.

## Conversations:

☐☐☐☐ Student demonstrates appropriate turn taking while conversing with others in 4/5 opportunities.

☐☐☐☐ Student independently greets others at appropriate times in 4/5 opportunities.

☐☐☐☐ Student independently says bye to others at appropriate times in 4/5 opportunities.

☐☐☐☐ Student is able to stay on topic when talking with others in 4/5 opportunities.

## Taking Care of Yourself:

☐☐☐☐ Student is able to demonstrate healthy habits by independently washing hands and coming to school in clean clothes in 4/5 opportunities.

☐☐☐☐ Student is able to ask for help when they are in need in 4/5 opportunities.

☐☐☐☐ Student shares appropriate information with the appropriate people in 4/5 opportunities.

☐☐☐☐ Student demonstrates self-control when in stressful situations in 4/5 opportunities.

## Self-Awareness and Self-Control

☐☐☐☐ Student is able to handle unexpected changes in their schedule without becoming overwhelmed in 4/5 opportunities.

☐☐☐☐ Student can identify and use appropriate coping skills when they become frustrated in 4/5 opportunities.

☐☐☐☐ Student is able to identify events that are likely to cause them stress in 4/5 opportunities.

☐☐☐☐ Student is able to remain composed when things don't go the way they want in 4/5 opportunities.

## Being Polite:

☐☐☐☐ Student is able to sensor their comments so they aren't offensive when conversing with others in 4/5 opportunities.

☐☐☐☐ Student holds the door for others around them without prompts in 4/5 opportunities.

☐☐☐☐ Student says please and thank you when others do things for them in 4/5 opportunities.

☐☐☐☐ Student is able to identify the difference between being polite and lying in 4/5 opportunities.

## Being Respectful:

☐☐☐ Student is able to use school property without damaging it in 4/5 opportunities.

☐☐☐ Student is able to respect the space of the students around them by only using their designated area in 4/5 opportunities.

☐☐☐ Student is able to show they are listening when others are talking by looking at them and paying attention in 4/5 opportunities.

☐☐☐ Student is able to refrain from interrupting others in non-emergency situations in 4/5 opportunities.

## Cooperation and Teamwork:

☐☐☐ Student independently initiates play with classmates in 4/5 opportunities.

☐☐☐ Student is able to complete group assignments without arguing in 4/5 opportunities.

☐☐☐ Student is able to take constructive criticism from others without being rude in 4/5 opportunities.

☐☐☐ When working on group assignments, student actively participates and contributes in 4/5 opportunities.

## Expressing Needs:

☐☐☐ Student is able to appropriately express needs when they are upset in 4/5 opportunities.

☐☐☐ Student chooses to ask others for assistance rather than sit and wait for someone to notice they need help in 4/5 opportunities.

☐☐☐ Student is able to express when they are feeling discomfort in an appropriate manner in 4/5 opportunities.

☐☐☐ Student is able to appropriately communicate what they need when things don't go as expected in 4/5 opportunities.

## Connecting with Others:

☐☐☐ Student addresses others by their name while interacting in 4/5 opportunities.

☐☐☐ When given a choice, student will choose to play with peers in 4/5 opportunities.

☐☐☐ Student will appropriately interact with a peer for 5 or more minutes in 4/5 opportunities.

☐☐☐ Student is able to show interest in others when having a conversation by asking questions relevant to the topic in 4/5 opportunities.

# Summary of Results

Pre-Assessment

☐ _____ :  Administrator _____

_____
_____
_____

End of Term 1

☐ _____ :  Administrator _____

_____
_____
_____

End of Term 2

☐ _____ :  Administrator _____

_____
_____
_____

End of Term 3

☐ _____ :  Administrator _____

_____
_____
_____

End of Term 4

☐ _____ :  Administrator _____

_____
_____
_____

Made in the USA
Lexington, KY
11 April 2014